HABITS

Six Steps to the Art of Influence

Marcus Goodie Goodloe, Ph.D.

Octavio Cesar Martinez

Printed in the United States of America
2017 First Edition
10 9 8 7 6 5 4 3 2 1

Subject Index:
Goodloe, Marcus Goodie and Martinez, Octavio Cesar
Title: H.A.B.I.T.S: Six Steps to the Art of Influence
1. Christian   2.Inspirational   3. Self-Help   4. Leadership   5. Business   6. Transformation

Paperback ISBN: 978-0-9964467-1-6
Library of Congress Card Catalog : 2017916221
Author Photo Credit: Steve Albano Photography
Cover Design Credit: Nick Macedo
Layout Design Credit: Ed Matte

Dream Life Loud LLC
424 North Broadway - #D
Redondo Beach, CA 90027

Website: www.habitsthebook.com

KUDOS TO SOUL-GUIDING HABITS...

"*HABITS* presents us with an opportunity to think differently about leadership. Goodloe and Martinez go beyond the familiar lists of skill sets and popular conceptions of success in favor of strategies grounded in the authentic health and wellness of the leader. The stories they share demonstrate the importance of cultivating the discipline to think and act in a values-driven and generous way. Collaboration and innovation are sure to follow as a result. It's a refreshing and empowering take on leadership — whether you're taking on a leadership role for the first time or you're a seasoned pro, *HABITS* is compelling!"

Dr. Karen Eshoo
Head of School
Vistamar School

"The life of Dr. Marcus 'Goodie' Goodloe absolutely radiates with conviction and purpose, and it comes through in every page of *HABITS: Six Steps to the Art of Influence*. Goodie's experience and intuition bring a refreshing perspective to our understanding of modern leadership. The profiles of men and women found in *HABITS* also reinforce the truth that leadership is developed through discipline, but is sustained through choices that enable everyone to be a person of influence. Whatever your vocation, if you seek a clear path to consistent leadership, I highly recommend this book!"

Steve Kelly
Senior Pastor
Wave Church

"Through life's hard lessons and God's compassionate love, Dr. Goodloe expresses what it really takes to be a leader. As influencers, *HABITS: Six Steps to the Art of Influence*, reminds us that leadership is a selfless act that consists of constant self-evaluations, and most importantly, taking the role of leadership seriously. It is a gift after all...and as such it must be cherished by all those entrusted with its power and potential."

Michelle Carter
3-time Olympian and 2016 Gold Medalist

"Practical, insightful and an influential book by a leader of great influence! Dr. Goodloe's charisma and wisdom shine through in this excellent work sure to inspire others to realize greater potential in themselves while transforming the world around them through simple actions resulting in profound impact."

Dr. Adam C. Wright
President of Dallas Baptist University

"Leadership is more art than science, which means people who wish to or do influence others must have a nimbleness of mind, character toward growth, and a sharp set of skills to engage in a dance toward goals and mission. HABITS has a trove of real-world wisdom that focuses on the realities of personal leadership and life, which are at the core of honest and successful leadership and influence. Readers will gain much wisdom, the practical 'stuff' that is important both in self-leadership and in influencing others."

Dr. David Gonzalez, Jr.
Assistant Professor of Public Administration &
Organizational Leadership

"Goodie and Octavio are tested leaders who have led in the trenches and are now using their experiences to help train and develop other leaders. HABITS is an easy to read, practical book that will help you to be more intentional in the development of your leadership. You'll want to start putting these habits into practice immediately. If you lead others, do yourself a favor and invest in your own leadership development by engaging in these six influence-shaping habits."

Mike Goldsworthy
Lead Pastor, Parkcrest Christian Church
Author of *In God We Trust? When the Kingdom of God and Politics Collide*

"Dr. Goodloe never ceases to amaze me with his insightful teachings, and *HABITS: Six Steps to the Art of Influence* is no exception. This book shines a light on the importance of building daily habits and shows us that without self reflection and acknowledgement of daily rituals, we may miss our divine destiny."

Angela Cannon
VP Content Distribution & Marketing UPTV & Aspire Author

"Goodie Goodloe brings the juice! His life represents each of these six *HABITS*. His friendship and influence have shaped my coaching style as well as my life as a husband, father, and friend. Tips for developing the HABITS you need in order to lead and influence at a high level are waiting in the chapters ahead. Remember, after you have read and learned you must consistently ACT!"

Zac Woodfin
Head Strength and Conditioning Coach
The University of Kansas

"HABITS is excellent reading for leaders desiring to extend their reach and influence in life. I enthusiastically recommend and endorse its message not just for those called to leadership in large organizations, businesses, and institutions, but for developing the God-given gift of leadership in all of us. Habits shape the way one leads, and effective leadership follows habits. Habits, performed consistently and practiced daily, enable effective and life-changing leadership to come forth. This is not just another self-help book to improve one's skills, but a way of life, complete with authentic stories both cultural and biblical, that will make a difference in the world."

Bishop W. Earl Bledsoe
New Mexico/Northwest Texas Conferences
The United Methodist Church

"I have worked in leadership development with Octavio both in Europe and in the US, with leaders from around the world. He is an extraordinary speaker with a tremendous ability to tell stories in such a way that draws every listener into a journey with him. Both his successes and his failures have contributed to his ability to lead with excellence and have given him the kind of experience needed to help others in their own path of development. I am glad that he has finally put into words some of the principles forged in his journey to make the world a better place.

Recognizing that my habits are just 'what I usually do' and that these things have a direct influence on my emotional, mental, physical and spiritual well-being, won me over to rethink some of my own habits and inspired me to seek healthy ones. As I went through the steps, I could picture Octavio in every one of them. He is writes from his own personal experience, and it was no surprise to me that step number one calls us to 'have fun.' This is what always brought a fresh breath of energy whenever we worked together."

Adaumir Nascente
Director of Care Operations
Unitymedia, Germany

"The ethos of *HABITS* will substantially impact practices in both small and affluent spaces. Dr. Goodloe calls us to take responsibility and examine our daily patterns as foundational to the formation of our communal influence. We learn that our habits can provide us with intentional pathways to success and triumph in both the physical and spiritual world."

Noemi Chavez
Lead Pastor
7th Street Church

"An excellent challenge to enjoy the beauty of life. With every page I felt more encouraged to develop sustainable habits and motivated to cultivate a positive and supportive ethos."

Dr. Uli Marienfeld
Director Christburg Campus
Berlin, Germany

"A wise and highly readable manifesto on the necessity of healthy habits for a full and good human life. Highly recommended."

Thomas M. Crisp, Ph.D.
Professor of Philosophy
Biola University

"Authentic, convicting, and practical. I have seen and experienced the principles outlined in this book demonstrated first-hand in Octavio's life over the past 30 years. I look back at the day I met him in 1987 and know with certainty that it was one of the most pivotal introductions in my life — a relationship began and the author began a journey with me that in hindsight, has been one of the most impactful and influential in all aspects of my life. Whether you are a seasoned professional or an individual looking for direction in life, the pragmatic tenets found within this book will provide the fresh direction, be it personally or professionally, that you have been looking for."

Anthony Valentino, Th.M.
Information Technology Director

"Influence remains an invaluable yet elusive commodity in our world. Even still, Goodie and Octavio share practical ways to acquire and maximize influence. I'm grateful for the opportunity I've had to serve personally with these two men who positively influenced me, and now with their book *HABITS*, their insights can inspire and equip you as well."

Dr. Eric Bryant, Pastor at Gateway Church, Austin
Author: *Not Like Me: Learning to Love, Serve, and Influence Our Divided World*
www.ericbryant.org

"Goodloe and Martinez have crafted a truly helpful guide to an abundant life of serving the world by influencing ourselves and others for good. They organize their thinking about the acronym *HABITS* to help in your transformation. They distill their wisdom in a winsome style rooted in their combined half-century of leadership experience. They use personal stories to illustrate each step toward becoming the people we were created to be. They also weave in a subtle, but rich thread of spirituality. This is a book worthy of a wide audience. Sign me up for a life shaped by *HABITS*!"

Brian D. Russell, Ph.D.
Associate Provost and Dean of the School of Urban Ministries
Professor of Biblical Studies
Asbury Theological Seminary

"Habits" is a common word that most people want to avoid because it may require change from an unhealthy thing or characteristic that is hindering their growth and development. If you are willing to embrace and practice the habits outlined in this book, you are bound to have more positive outcomes in your personal relationships and your impact on the lives of others.

"Regardless of your leadership level or role of influence, *HABITS: Six Steps to the Art of Influence*, provides practical insight to impact your life by exposing key areas in human interactions that most of us struggle to balance or exhibit. Every page brings you to a point of self-reflection in your daily life and putting the "Habits" recommended into use will most certainly change your life."

Cesar Marrufo
Telecommunications Industry Executive
Greater Los Angeles

"Octavio practices what he preaches. His book encourages all of us to look at the big picture of our life and what direction we are headed in. Want to change your life? Change your habits moment by moment. I love that he encourages us to have fun in the process. With all the work being done in the science of well-being, Octavio delivers a usable formula for happiness and success in life."

Joseph Valentine Dworak
Senior Business Development Lead & Consultant
Leadership Vision | Minneapolis, MN

"Octavio Martinez's eclectic curiosity and genuine warmth shine through every page of this book, offering the reader encouragement, insight, and practical steps toward creating a better future. With powerful storytelling and honest questions, *HABITS* is an experienced look at the discipline of influencing others."

Kevin Knox
Author of *No Matter What* and Pastor of Mosaic Bay Church

DEDICATION

To Chester French Stewart. I am grateful beyond measure for your care and compassion. Thanks for your admonishment, support, wisdom, investment, encouragement, and these last twenty-five years of what it means to be a mentor and now, father.

Marcus Goodie Goodloe

To my parents Octavio and Carmen, whom I love and miss every day.

Octavio Cesar Martinez

TABLE OF CONTENTS

A NOTE FROM THE AUTHORS

All of the stories represented in this book are based on actual events. Names and identifying details have been changed to protect individual privacy.

INTRODUCTION

"HABITS is an anecdotal project based upon our own experiences, circumstances, and faith. It is our interpretation of what the best leaders are made of, drawn from a combined 50 plus years of leading and being led."

The most important point we want you to get out of this book is this: **You are the sum total of the habits you create, both good and bad.** Habits forge pathways that will shape your future and the future of those you lead, love, and serve alongside. What you do with your skills, talent, time, and other human resources matters. There are profound implications if you fail to consider what you are becoming by virtue of what you are doing, day in, day out. The results of your habits are not abstract or ethereal. They are concrete: observable and obvious. Your habits create the texture, tone, and temperament of your life—whether you lead thousands of people, or two people.

This book is not simply for leaders. Rather, it speaks to the leader inside all of us: that part of the self that desires to use your influence, skills, talents, and gifts to make the lives of others better. We believe that the term "leader" is interchangeable with "influencer"—and we all have influence. Although we have incorporated leadership concepts throughout the book, you don't need to be employed as a top level manager to benefit from its pages. In the same way, although we use scriptural references, you don't have to be religious to glean wisdom from the true stories in this book. You are bound to see yourself in several of the narratives—and we welcome you to consider what they might have to say to you.

Consider these questions:

When was the last time you made time to help someone out?

When was the last time you felt pure joy in helping someone else?

When did you last take time to have fun?

These questions are less about you remembering the facts you need in order to answer, and more about pressing into whether or not a certain type of reality exists in your ethos and mindset: a reality where having fun, helping others, and living life to the fullest are part of the natural rhythm of your life.

Over the course of our lives, we have been afforded opportunities to meet some extraordinary people: leaders of academic institutions, faith communities, and businesses; as well as working moms, stay-at-home dads, artists, athletes, scientists, law enforcement officials, and political activists. Our conversations with each of them have been etched into the sacred parts of our hearts. We have been inspired by their stories and overwhelmed by their capacity to lead, serve, and sacrifice for the good of others. Most importantly, we have seen them lead, serve, and sacrifice with pure joy.

Despite the differences reflected by each of them—their political views, the color of their skin, their life experiences, where they were born and where they live—they are all effective, well-regarded leaders. Their leadership styles are different and their skills are vastly diverse. Yet there is one factor that remains true among those who lead with an aim to serve others.

They have habits.

Healthy habits.

Healthy habits are activities you engage in that are beneficial to your emotional, mental, physical and spiritual well-being. Healthy habits require a strong commitment and a high level of discipline.

Your habits allow you to formulate consistency in the things you do well. As your habits develop, your leadership will follow. The results cannot be overstated. Rather than arriving at moments of excellence by chance, your potential for success can be charted and measured based upon your patterns and activities. At any given moment, you have the capacity to fall short of your God-given potential. The likelihood of falling short, however, decreases dramatically when you form healthy habits — ones that are noble, honorable, generous; habits that take into account who you can become.

"Habits, scientists say, emerge because the brain is constantly looking for ways to save effort."
-Charles Duhigg

Healthy habits are the fuel that moves leaders from mediocrity to greatness. They are natural rhythms that are less about ritual, and more about constants that serve as anchor points to help leaders navigate. Habits are what spiritual giants who study the scriptures call disciplines: noted practices, lived out daily, leading to established characteristics that are seen, felt, and heard. What may appear to be a fluke of success or effectiveness, is in reality a discipline that leaders have spent time developing and growing. Areas such as prayer, reflection, meditation, and silence are spiritual disciplines. Each of these is a cornerstone in the life of a person who desires to live and serve the Creator with purpose and passion. Successful leaders embrace habits that not only influence and impact their achievements, but the success of those they lead.

As we talk about habits, we have to acknowledge that the word "habit" often comes with negative connotations. To some extent, a negative reaction isn't unfounded. At times, habits can be destructive. Just look at how we usually use the word: We admonish others not to pick up bad habits from the wrong people. We say we're "creatures of habit" as an excuse for our lack of change. We talk about how things would be different, if only we could kick that bad habit.

And it's not just us. Bad habits are part of the story of our nation. Unfortunately, our eating habits as a country are not healthy. Millions of people choose to eat recklessly, often ignoring the adverse health consequences of high blood pressure, heart disease, diabetes, and obesity. Likewise, smoking is an addictive habit. Research shows that it causes cancer and a host of other health problems. Local laws seek to limit people from smoking in just about every public space imaginable. Yet, tobacco usage remains high, and in some instances, fashionable. Why? It's a habit.

Smoking, overeating — these are habits we want to get rid of. Bad habits do nothing to add value to your life, or to the lives of those around you. But what about good habits? What if doing something over and over again was a good thing? What if it could set you up for success, for becoming your best self? What if you spent energy building healthy habits instead of trying to get rid of bad ones? We may need to readjust our automatic negative reaction to the word "habits."

There's no getting around the fact that developing good habits will add value to your life. In his *New York Times* bestseller, *The Power of Habit*, Charles Duhigg described a three-step "Habit Loop" to demonstrate how we develop habits. First, there is a *Cue* to trigger our response to do something. Then our *Response* is automatic. Finally, we are excited to receive our *Reward*. The good news is that scientific research shows you can change your unhealthy habits into good ones. The key is to change the way you respond to the *cues* that trigger a bad habit. For instance, if you have a habit of snacking on junk food when you feel stressed or just crave a snack, you should restock your pantry full of chocolatey treats and salty pretzels with healthier snacks like granola bars and veggie chips. Better yet, place a bowl of fresh fruit on your counter or in the refrigerator. Over time, when your body receives a cue for a snack, you will automatically grab a piece of fruit or reach for a healthier snack from the pantry. Why not implement a new routine or activity that allows you to become your best self? Make today your "Aha!" moment to expand and grow your healthy habits.

We hope this book will lead you to the moments of reflection you need to begin establishing your own healthy habits. There are six chapters, presented as steps. Each step should lead you into implementing that specific habit in your daily life. Step One, *Have Fun*, examines the idea and practice of embracing every moment as a gift from the Creator. It calls you to consider the passion and potential of your life when you make time to celebrate life — and everything in between. Step Two, *Assume the Best of Others*, considers the endless possibilities that lie in the human story when we take time to engage one another, not based on a perception or past experience, but from a present, genuine interaction. Step Three, *Be Good Soil*, is the posture of being a continuous learner and receiver of good seed, which is a key characteristic of leadership. Being good soil embraces an optimistic mindset: if something can advance your life, then you should always be open to a new learning experience.

In Step Four, *Insist Upon Excellence*, we examine what it looks like to not only produce a fine product or presentation, but to be the best version of ourselves. When we insist upon excellence, we accept the process as well as the end result. Step Five, *Treat Others as Sacred*, advances the idea that leaders should hold the needs of those they lead in high regard. Such needs being met for others is tantamount to an act of worship and reverence. This chapter also expands upon this similar concept first advanced by scholar Obery Hendricks, who examined the life and teachings of Jesus in his book, *The Politics of Jesus*. Finally, Step Six, *Seek Community*, issues a clarion call to leaders that effective leadership is never done in isolation, but in the context of community. It focuses on the importance of relationship and what it looks like to advance both your personal life and leadership life through a commitment to community.

It is our desire that this book will prompt you to begin developing healthy habits—ones that set others up for success and establish a legacy of selflessness, producing good for all those you influence. It takes diligence. It requires intention. It demands sacrifice. The stakes are high, yet it's within your control. It's your body, mind and soul. Let the transformation begin!

"Transformation is much more than using skills, resources and technology. It is all about habits of mind."

-Malcolm Gladwell

HAVING FUN IS THE ART
OF NOT TAKING YOURSELF
TOO SERIOUSLY.

HABITS LEGEND

 H=Have Fun

 A=Assume the Best in Others

 B = Be Good Soil

 I= Insist Upon Excellence

 T= Treat Others as Sacred

 S= Seek Community

STEP 1

HAVE FUN

What fun elements play into your approach when leading others?

Think about it — when *was* the last time you had fun? Last week? Last year? Last...decade? Maybe you even have to think back all the way to your childhood before you can come up with an example.

We probably don't have to tell you that adult life is challenging and stressful. Medical science tells us that when we're stressed, our bodies release hormones[1] which can hinder our ability to fight infection, leading to illness. Unbalanced hormones can also cause weight gain, stress, depression, and sleeplessness. No big surprises there. You probably also know that there are amazing health benefits associated with having fun — it triggers quite different chemicals in the body, which help boost our memory, and regulate our sleeping patterns, coping skills, and our overall mood.

So what's stopping you from having fun? Just knowing that stress is bad for you and fun is good for you doesn't get the job done. There has to be a connection between knowledge and behavior. As strange as it may sound, we have to make having fun a priority. We must build habits of having fun.

Play Like No One is Watching

"Having fun is the art of not taking yourself too seriously."

As Kevin settled in on his flight from New Orleans to Los Angeles, he looked across the aisle and saw a boy traveling alone. The young man must have been around thirteen years old; small in stature, but with an evident air of confidence. Based on where he was seated, and the identification placard displayed around his neck, it was clear that he was flying solo—but Kevin got the sense this kid had been on a flight before.

Just then, a woman boarded the plane. Since she was at least six feet tall, no one would have faulted her for choosing one of the available aisle seats, but instead, she decided to sit next to the boy across the aisle from Kevin. After making small talk with the flight attendant, the woman began to engage the young boy. If Kevin hadn't seen their initial interaction and greeting, he would have thought they'd known each other for years. Prior to boarding, Kevin had made a commitment to himself: he needed to take this flight to catch up on sleep after several weeks on the road. Yet his attention was drawn to this young teen and a six-foot-tall total stranger who decided to sit next to him.

Kevin was in awe. The woman was in full play mode. She asked the boy questions, and they played a round of what appeared to be Rock, Paper, Scissors. To Kevin's amazement, he saw her share her (very expensive) all-natural almonds with the teen. The woman then took out her phone and began sharing what looked like photos of her family. Kevin was fascinated. Getting little sleep, and no work done, he found himself watching the two of them: totally immersed in conversation, laughing and talking like old friends.

After the first leg of the flight ended, everyone deplaned for the connecting flight. Kevin arrived at his connecting gate, and who did he see but the six-foot-tall woman from the previous flight. She too was headed to Los Angeles. He felt compelled to ask her about her interaction with the boy. He went over, introduced himself, and commented on what he had observed on the previous flight, offering her warranted and unmeasured praise. Initially, she seemed taken aback. First, that anyone noticed, and second, that he took the time to say thank you on behalf of the young man. The woman confirmed that she had never met him prior to the flight, but felt led to sit next to him, even at the expense of compromising leg room.

When Kevin pressed her for why she did what she did, she paused and simply said, "It's who I am. I like to help people. I love to have fun. It's a good habit I've had all my life!" What she said resonated with Kevin. He realized that her response was the essence of how he desired to live his life: to help people, to have fun, and more importantly, to make a habit of doing so, for the good of himself and others.

BUILDING HABITS

- When was the last time you had fun?
- How often do you make fun a priority?
- What are some ways you can build fun into your life as a habit?
- List three activities that would be fun for a group you're part of (your work colleagues, a community organization, a small group Bible study, a team you lead, your family or circle of friends).
- Present your ideas the next time you get together.

If You're Happy and You Know It

"It is the ultimate luxury to combine passion and contribution. It's also a very clear path to happiness."

-Sheryl Sandberg

Only happy people actually have fun. Wealth and money rarely have anything to do with having fun and experiencing happiness.[2] No matter what you wear, where you work, what you drive, where you live or how much you weigh, you can learn to have fun and be happy. Having fun is tied to happiness, and happiness is a choice. Period.

One of the key sources of happiness is gratitude: learning to be grateful for everything—big or small.

Octavio:

"Can I speak to you for a minute? In the conference room."

Bob was my boss's boss. A second level manager. He was about 5 feet 7 inches tall, and always wore his hair in a classic side part. Without fail, Bob wore a brownish suit, a solid tie with a crisp white shirt, and polished... wait for it... brown wing tips. He was the perfect blend between Bill Murray and Dean Martin in his walk, demeanor and diction. Perpetually upbeat and funny. Except, not right then.

When you're in your twenties, you think you know everything about anything. I was no different. I read *TIME, Newsweek, US News & World Report,* and about one book of non-fiction every month. Later, I would move to reading one book a week. I thought information made me wise. Nope. It made me a smart-mouth and a know-it-all.

I was a handful to management, and I'm surprised I wasn't fired for insubordination. To be fair, I was a decent employee who could complete tasks quickly with little supervision and few customer complaints. Maybe that's why they put up with me. But Bob was a grown man who was too decent to take my crap.

So he didn't.

I confidently followed Bob into the conference room, and he closed the door behind me. "I'll deny this conversation if you file a grievance," he said, with none of his usual pleasantness. This was a union shop and the interaction was way out of protocol. "Sit down," he said. I sat down. Then Bob did me one of the biggest favors of my life. He spoke directly to me, man-to-man, and he put me in his place.

"You know, Octavio, you're not under contract," he said. "You can go anytime you want. If you're not happy, be brave enough to leave. Life's too short to work at a place where you're not happy."

I was stunned. He turned to the door, but paused for one last shot. "Take all the time you need, but do not leave this room until you have decided to stay or leave," he said over his shoulder.

That was my last day.

That exchange with Bob left a lasting impression, and yet it took me a while to find a job that was a better fit. I knew I was essentially unhappy on the inside, but I didn't realize exactly why until later: I had made the classic, common, chronic mistake of believing happiness was found in external circumstances instead of inner character. What was the key missing ingredient in my character?

Gratitude.

"Gratitude and happiness are inseparable."

One of the most vital characteristics of human flourishing is gratitude. To practice gratitude is to learn to be fearless and generous.

Eric is a young man who was talking about suicide with a frequency that alarmed his friends. He was living abroad and reached out to a mutual friend for help. As he talked about his unhappiness and desire to end his life, it was clear that most of all, Eric needed friends to care about him. But given the distance, it was difficult for him to find the connection he needed at that moment.

This mutual friend asked Eric to try something out: "Take a picture of one thing you find beautiful every day. It doesn't matter what it is. Email me the image and tell me why you think it's beautiful."

The first week, he took photos of dead birds and debris. By the second week, he began to take photos of parks, flowers, and kids playing. Before the month ended, Eric's outlook was completely different. He began to see that happiness was not a zero-sum game. He realized that he could be happy with his life if he chose to be.

But how did he get there?

Beauty.

He started to look at the beauty around him, he began to want a beautiful life, and then he began to understand that happiness started with him. Beauty has a way of charming us, wooing us, and calling us to discover and understand something true about ourselves and about the world. Confronting and recognizing beauty creates gratitude. And gratitude will generate happiness. In this way, experiencing beauty is healing.

Bishop Robert Barron put it another way:

> The pattern is more or less as follows: first the beautiful (how wonderful!), then the good (I want to participate!) and finally the true (now I understand!). A young man watches a skillfully played game of baseball, and it awakens in him a profound desire to play as well as those whom he admired; and then the actual playing of the game teaches him, from

the inside, the rules and rhythms of baseball. A completely inadequate way of drawing a kid into the world of baseball would be to start with a clarification of the rules or with a set of drills. Rather, show him the beauty of baseball, and he will want to play, and having played, he will know. [3]

Eric needed to experience beauty in order to be transformed by it. And his experience of beauty began to grow gratitude within. As we've said earlier, happiness is directly linked to gratitude. One feeds the other in lifting you out of the unhealthy, unhappy life you've been living. Have fun (be happy) by learning to be grateful.

So if you're not happy,
if you're not having fun,
change it.
Start with you.
Be grateful.
Be happy.
Or at least happier.
And less of a jerk.

We are as happy as we choose to be.
So, while you work, play, or pray...have fun.

BUILDING HABITS

- Are you a happy person? Would people who know you well say you are a happy person?
- Are you a grateful person? Do you see all your benefits?

If you answered NO to any of these questions, try this:

1. Write down one thing you are grateful for each day.

2. Point out what is good in your home, your work, or your commute.

3. Refuse to linger on a negative emotion or moment.

Stop and Smell the Roses

Goodie:

Five days a week, my wife and I are privileged to do something most families are not afforded the luxury of doing: picking up their kids from school. We not only pick them up from school; we literally pick them up less than 1,000 yards from our front door. After a few steps up the sidewalk, we turn the corner, trek one block east, and we are at their bus stop. When the kids step off the bus, they can see us in the distance as we walk.

These days, we've grown accustomed to what we call the law of diminishing affection. When the kids were young, they'd run to greet us, giving warm and fuzzy kisses, full-fledged hugs, breathless embraces. Now, we're thankful for a couple of high fives. The kids hand over their backpacks, followed by questions about how soon dinner will be ready. But without fail, there is one thing we insist that we do as a family — one walking-home activity we've made a habit. (It even takes precedent over forced hugs.) I have my kids join me to stop and smell the roses.

Just down the street from the bus stop is a house with a white fence and a bed of red roses that grow to hang just over the fence line. When the flowers are in full bloom, they call out to be noticed, embraced, and loved. And we take the time to do just that: notice those roses. We enjoy the color and smell the aroma that permeates the immediate surroundings. It's become a habit. We stop to smell the roses. After all these years, we are still in awe of the vibrancy, color, smell, and texture of a rose. Roses are life-giving and eye-appealing; their beauty and presence demand our attention. And for me and my tribe, nothing less than our full attention is given.

Stopping to smell the roses is a good habit — an invaluable, free, "Have Fun" habit. It's also a way of staying in the moment, of being present, of resetting your perspective so that you notice the gifts that are all around you. Regardless of the circumstances you are facing, this is a habit that you can practice without much effort.

To demonstrate this point, Laura Kubzansky, Associate Professor of Society, Human Development and Health, has spent years researching the scientific and biological effects of the positive attitude. The heart of her research is the crux of this habit. "Everyone needs to find a way to be in the moment," she says, "to find a restorative state that allows them to put their burdens down."[4]

If Kubzansky's research is true, we don't have any more excuses about being too busy to stop and smell the roses. Whether you are unhappy with your chosen career or just weighed down by life's challenges, now is the opportune time to stop, take a deep breath and have fun. Taking time to notice the beauty around you — to literally stop and smell the roses — will open your heart and soul to the moment you're in right now. It will lessen the weight of worrying about tomorrow, and might be one of the most influential habits you can incorporate into your daily routine. We are convinced that we must all live in a way that allows for — even plans — moments where life is cherished as a gift, and celebrated one breath at a time. Having fun doesn't take a lot of money. It doesn't even take a lot of time. However, it does require you to be fully present.

> *"Happiness is not something you postpone for the future,*
> *it is something you design for the present."*
> **-Jim Rohn**

Embracing the "have fun" habit is more than a singular event; it's a posture, a mindset, and an attitude of the heart. In order to move forward by having fun, you have to be intentional. Whatever your daily role requires, intentionality is everything. If you are not intentional about setting goals for yourself or your team, then you are an ineffective leader. Having fun must become part of your way of life. So what does that look like — practically speaking? Start with scheduling. At the end of the day, leaders expend time and focus on things they do well. If you are good at golf, schedule time to play a few rounds with a few people you know who are interested in playing. Maybe most of your team isn't interested in golf (or you're not!). Find something that the majority is interested in doing, and implement it as a group activity. The goal is to be intentional, listen to your team, and make time to have fun together.

Sights To Be Seen

When was the last time you took a scenic drive? As native Californians we've driven along the coast in Palos Verdes, California countless times. The views of the bluest ocean and abundant waves are nothing short of breathtaking. Most mornings there are surfers trying to catch perfect waves, seabirds making their morning voyage, and whales or dolphins just hanging out within view. There are days you can actually see dolphins jumping out of the water!

On these scenic drives, it can be easy to let the beauty become commonplace. It is so important to take it all in — to enjoy what's in front of you, and to not take what you are seeing, smelling, hearing, and feeling for granted. Of course, if you are the driver, you must be careful to be present in watching the road, as well as present in the beauty of the moment! Maybe you don't have a glorious coastal drive nearby, but you can schedule time in your week to take scenic strolls in parks, gardens, or to visit other natural wonders.

This is the essence of the first letter of Habits: Have Fun. Having fun is more than a moment of glee. It is an expression of gratitude and a time where you become keenly aware that what you are experiencing is a first and a last. Having fun is an awareness that what's in front of you is a gift from the Creator: the colors, sounds, textures, and landscapes around you warrant your undivided attention.

The skies are not bland, nor is the ocean devoid of vitality, color, and life. Sunrises are not lacking in the spectacular, and you'd be hard-pressed to find someone who has seen an "average" sunset. These are not moments to capture a selfie — they are about an escape to witness something greater than yourself. Take it all in, by yourself or with others.

BUILDING HABITS

- When was the last time you watched a sunset? Stopped to smell a rose peeking over a fence, or play a spontaneous game of catch?

- Have you ever taken interest in the smell of fresh baked bread?

- Did you ever take time to observe the flight patterns of birds as they streak across the sky?

- Try to commit to noticing and enjoying these things—on your own or as a family.

Play Dates

"Play dates are the permission to make time for yourself and to include others in the journey as you explore your block, your city, state, our nation, and even the world."

"Play dates" seem to be part of the universal language of being a parent. However, play dates don't have to be just for your kids. As we urge you to build a habit of having fun in your life, we want to dispel the myth that play is reserved exclusively for children. However, remembering how you played as a kid is valuable as you consider how to build fun into your life as an adult.

Think back to when you were younger. The term "play dates" is fairly new but the intention was exactly the same, even 50 years ago. Recall how you and your buddies developed friendships, created imaginary worlds, and discovered things about each other in the context of vibrant play dates that would not have happened if they had been scheduled. It was effortless, ongoing, and beautiful. You might have played tag football, hide and go seek, or worked on your baseball skills. Maybe you created imaginary scenarios, casting yourselves as the stars in the final innings of a Major League World Series. Playing together with your friends was where the magic happened! You made time for each other, and you were never short of new adventures to imagine, experience, and share with each other.

Play is part of the innate, common language and rhythm of every human being, and we are convinced that play dates should become part of the official language—not just of parents with young children—but of us all.

Play dates are where you imagine making the game-winning shot; discover what it means to breathe again, to love and be loved, to forgive and be forgiven. There are back yards waiting to be discovered and explored, and those back yards have relationships and connections to others that are more vibrant than the summer fruit eaten from a tree. Play dates are one of the best options you have to discover who you are and what you are invited to become when you place your trust and life in the hands of the Transcendent.

Take time to escape from the mundane and the predictable. Accept this formal invitation to live outside the realm of the 9-to-5, and instead move to the rhythm of life. Sometimes that rhythm says to slow down, reflect, and consider how blessed you are. And sometimes that rhythm says to get up and dance! Restrictions for embodying this habit are few, yet this is where your character is formed. It's where you gain a deep sense of appreciation for life, and for living it more abundantly. Play dates are an opportunity to discover that you have been given some of the most important resources on the planet: creativity, passion, and time. What defines you as a leader is how you use these resources — where, when and how often you play is often what separates good leaders from great leaders. Find your back yard, schedule a play date, and move forward in creating a world that is in desperate need of beauty.

Here is where we see the practical expression of the habit of having fun. Venture out to discover a love for foods you are not accustomed to eating, interact with people from different cultures, and embrace sights and sounds outside of your usual experiences. Check out your local hotspot's special deal. Whether it's Monday Madness with crazy fries or Tuesday's 2-for-$2 ice cream floats, take the time to celebrate the day with family and friends.

BUILDING HABITS

- Where is your local hotspot?
- What path will you take for today's group stroll?
- How can you recreate your childhood back yard?

Every Day is Happy Hour

Do Millennials really have more fun than Boomers, Gen X-ers or other generations? Maybe. It appears as though they have mastered the work/play balancing act. These young cool kids are drenched with skills and talents beyond measure. They work from sunup to sundown to advance their dreams, all while having fun in their offices or dens. A large part of this generation is determined to forge new ground, to bring creative, innovative ideas into reality. There is a present-day gold rush in the Silicon Valley of Northern California. But this startup gold rush has nothing to do with rocks in the ground. Millennials are the ringleaders of this startup culture.

Typically identified as being born between 1980 and 2004, Millennials account for roughly thirty percent of the United States' population. Millennial entrepreneurs are building apps and new technologies to fulfill their dreams and steer their own future. Take notes — because this startup culture knows the value of having fun! They've built it into their very workplaces. They have ping-pong and billiard tables in break rooms, in-house masseuses and fitness gyms, cafes offering energy drinks and specialty coffee — all within their workspace.

Gone are the days of traditional 9-to-5 work days. Instead, flex schedules rule the day, which makes organizations task-driven, not time-driven. Millennials are building and creating a host of ideas that have never before existed. This generation thrives on doing whatever it takes to advance their own interests, and the interests of their organizations. They are not working for a pay check per se, but are more interested in stock options. The end result of their work has the potential to cost them everything. Millennials have transformed business models and the approach to marketing for their dollars has been turned upside down. From the automotive industry, to home ownership, to science and technology and the arts, Millennials continue to cause seismic shifts in lifestyles and the way our world does business. Their driving common denominator is that they are committed to changing the world.

We can learn from this generation. Even with putting in long hours, they have found ways to have fun in the madness of a crazy work day. Not only do they work alongside their friends, but they have chosen to live life together as well. Friendship and fun is integrated into work in a way that makes it healthy. [5]

Millennials have built a culture of having fun in the midst of work. Yet, some of you reading this will have to actually *stop* working in order to smell the roses. Across the United States, from city to city and every place in between, we embrace the concept of **Happy** Hour. The idea is to take the time right after work to relax, unwind, and leave the stress and strain of the workplace behind. Restaurants and bars offer special menus and half-price drinks, attracting people who need an escape from the day-to-day grind. Happy Hour is a time to forget about what happened at work and let the fun begin! Now, it's not that millennials don't go to Happy Hour. Instead, they simply continue to have fun with the same colleagues they've just worked with all day. They are not trying to escape the workplace or their colleagues, but rather to cultivate and build on what they started over the course of the workday. They've built time into their workday to enjoy life, and that just continues when they leave the office.

One of the wisest choices we can make is to find something that forces us to stay in the moment. Instead of Millennials leaving their "workspace," they incorporate "the moment" into their work life. What Millennials have figured out is that when you mix these two—being in the moment and having fun—an extraordinary phenomena can take place: great productive work that you can be proud of at the end of the day. You don't need to stop work to have fun; instead you can find ways to incorporate fun into the context of the work you do. Might we suggest that if you don't have time to have fun during the course of a regular day, then perhaps you're in a role that's above your head? Can you afford to make time to reflect and enjoy what's in front of you?

 It's easy to become fascinated with the teachings of Jesus: his life, leadership practices, and compassion towards others. Every interaction Jesus had with others underscored not only his mission in life (to redeem humanity), but how he viewed life itself. The first miracle of Jesus ever recorded in the scripture occurred at a wedding. Jesus was undoubtedly among dozens if not hundreds of people in attendance. The wine ran out, and the reputation of both the host and the bride and groom's families was on the line. Jesus was informed of this dilemma by his mother, who accompanied him at this festive affair. Mary invited Jesus to do something to alleviate the growing problem, and to do so quickly.

A wedding in any culture is a big deal. But in the Jewish culture of the time, it could go on for days, if not weeks. Can you imagine the impression this embarrassment would have left on family members and guests? After some initial resistance by Jesus, he consented to his mother's request, and performed one of the most significant beer runs ever recorded in human history.

A few observations from this miraculous moment are in order. First, Jesus was invited to this wedding—and he attended. You'd think that of all the things he was compelled to give his attention to, attending a wedding celebration would not be at the top of his list. Not so with this first-century Jew from Palestine. Jesus was present, and our guess is that he was fully engaged. How do we know? There were people present—people from all walks, backgrounds, and experiences—and people were his number one priority.

Second, even though Jesus initially questioned his mother's request for him to do something about the wine running low, he eventually agreed. He had a plan and instructed the host's servants to follow it to the letter. They did, and the rest, as they say, is history. Water was turned into wine, and the batch Jesus created was better tasting than anything that had been on tap up until that point.

Third and finally, without over-spiritualizing this: Jesus kept the party going. We can assume the guests had fun. Running out of wine — and the guests becoming aware of it — would have been bad on so many levels. But Jesus saves the day (no pun intended). The celebration continued, and the people who attended the wedding not only saw the miracle of two people committing their lives to one another, influenced by love; they saw another miracle: turning water into wine.

Jesus kept people happy. Can you imagine that wedding being anything but fun? Two people committing their lives to each other is a thing of beauty, worthy of celebration. Jesus understood this and kept the celebration going. Having fun was not beyond the boundaries of Jesus' earthly job description.

There is no question that Jesus was on a mission. He had little patience for those who kept the rules but failed to exercise grace and kindness towards others. Jesus had more than enough occasions to express his anger, disappointment, and frustration over what he saw on a daily basis: women not given the dignity and respect due them as image-bearers of God; children tolerated rather than celebrated; the sick, disabled, and economically disenfranchised treated as less than. Learned men and teachers of Jewish law and traditions made it their mission to discredit Jesus. As a first-century carpenter and young man from Galilee, Jesus had a lot on his plate. Yet, he made time to attend a wedding, and to make sure that the joyous celebration continued when the drink became scarce. It's as if having fun was also part of Jesus' purpose and mission for his time on earth.

As you embark upon your life's mission — one that has focus and takes into consideration the significant things — do not forget to include the habit of having fun. It, too, is significant! Do whatever you need to do to keep the party going. Whatever is being asked or expected of you in the short term, as well as for the foreseeable future — remember to have fun. If Jesus did it, so can you!

There is still time.

Be grateful.
    Stop.
        Look.
            Listen.
                Smell.
                    Explore.
                        Fun awaits!

Yesterday's gone. Tomorrow is not promised. Be mindful of your health, your mortality. Prioritize, practice, and fully embrace the habit of having fun.

ASSUMING THE BEST IN OTHERS TAKES COURAGE. COWARDS NEED NOT APPLY.

STEP 2

HBITS

ASSUME THE BEST OF OTHERS

When you meet a person different from you, what does it take for you to assume the best in them?

Assuming the best of others is often challenging. Why? Because people are difficult. That's why organizations, businesses, churches, nonprofits, and families are messy; they contain people. Assuming the best of others takes courage. Cowards need not apply.

Deep down, we all fear the assumptions others make about us. And yet, we all do it. People begin to size each other up from the very first moment they begin to interact. Whether it's your voice on the phone, the way you dress, your hair color, hairstyle, weight, or body language—everyone you interact with draws several immediate conclusions about you based on one or more of these facets. And, no doubt—you do the same with them. Are these assumptions justified? Probably not!

> *"It's never too late to give up our prejudices."*
> **-Henry David Thoreau**

There is no doubt a sense of disappointment in being judged or made out to be someone you are not. The sting can linger in your soul like the smell of rotten fish. Even if a person's perception of you is valid in some areas, that does not give them the green light to write you off as strictly "this way" or "that way."

Our perceptions of others are ultimately just opinions. Those perceptions are not necessarily correct, yet judging others is instinctual. We can't help it. It's a bad habit that we must be cognizant of as soon as we look at someone and notice those wild and negative thoughts creeping in. Research conducted by the *Journal of Neuroscience* concluded that the brain immediately decides how trustworthy a face is—even before it is fully perceived. Indeed, we are very quick to make judgments about other people. [6]

BUILDING HABITS

- Do you think that people are basically bad and untrustworthy?

- Do you often make judgments based on "gut feeling"?

- Have you ever discovered—once you got to know someone—that you'd initially misjudged them?

If you answered YES to any of these questions, try this instead:

1. Assume that people are generally good and trustworthy — and that you'll like each other.
2. Make no permanent judgments based on feelings.
3. Take time to get to know someone who you'd initially written off.

"The soul tends to always judge others
by what it thinks of itself."
-Giacomo Leopardi

Judging on first sight is a negative habit that we should all strive to overcome. Whether we are uncomfortable with a person's race, ethnicity, or religion, we need to get with the program and work on becoming comfortable. There is enough psychological information to confirm that our discomfort with someone different from us, is a sign that we may have an unhealthy view of ourselves. Assuming the worst of others may say more about you than it does about them.

Think about what would happen if we approached every relationship at face value. If we were to start with a clean slate, to make a promise not to prejudge the person who sits across from us on the subway, or takes our order at a local coffee shop. Don't label every person who offers to help as a schemer, just because you were taken advantage of in the past. Not everyone is out to take something that belongs to you; either emotionally, physically or spiritually. Rather than immediately sizing others up, making quick judgments and assuming the worst, make a habit of assuming the best. Withhold judgment until you've had time to make an objective evaluation. Give yourself and others an opportunity to actually experience the different characteristics you each hold.

Goodie:

On a typical morning, I set out on a leisurely stroll to one of my favorite escapes: Whole Foods Market. All too often I go there and spend more money than I want. Whole Foods is like the amusement park of grocery stores—I see something that looks appealing, and I just have to try it! On this particular morning, I was heading home, walking along the sidewalk, and I noticed a woman coming towards me. I noticed her, but I don't know if she saw me noticing her. The reason I noticed her was that when I looked up, she was making a mini-sprint across the street.

The street was busy, and there was no crosswalk or light, so it took some serious navigation for her to avoid the traffic. I didn't give it much thought until a few seconds later, when I saw that the woman had returned to the same side of the street she'd just left. My side of the street. She continued on that same sidewalk until she turned a corner. In that moment, I knew what had happened— or so I am convinced. For whatever reason, she made a conscious decision to avoid walking past me. She changed her path in order to avoid crossing my path. I can't be certain of the her reasons, but to this day, I can remember how I felt and what I was left thinking.

Just a few months before that Whole Foods walk, I had another experience with assumptions that gave me pause. I was waiting at the bus stop as usual, to meet my kids after school, when a woman appeared seemingly out of nowhere and said "Hello." I replied in kind, and she asked if I needed anything. When I said "No, thank you," she asked if I lived nearby, and again, wondered aloud if I needed something. I initially thought she was being kind and friendly, but it slowly dawned on me what was behind her questions. I quickly told her I lived just up the block and that I was waiting to pick up my children. She stated that she meant no disrespect—but that lately people had been coming around the neighborhood who didn't belong; people who were up to no good. I was taken aback by her frankness, and found it difficult to hide my disappointment. She immediately began to backpedal, apologizing and offering other reasons for questioning me... but the damage was already done. My kids arrived, hopped off the bus, and hugged me. We headed home, and as we walked past the woman, our eyes met and I shook my head. I had no words. I still have no words. Why had she immediately assumed that I was up to no good, assumed that I didn't belong? Why was I the victim of someone assuming the worst of me?

No Favoritism

One of the most consistent baselines of our assumptions comes from the stigmas carried by race and ethnicity. The U.S. has a long and infamous history of treating people wrongly on this flawed basis. Fortunately, we have grown as a nation to some degree, but we still have a long way to go. As Dr. King so eloquently stated in his *I Have a Dream* speech, "one day we will live in a nation where our children will not be judged by the color of their skin, but by the content of their character."

 The Israelites of Jesus' day made their own judgments about people who were different from themselves. And yet, in the scriptures, we see Jesus engaging with others who were different from him; those individuals who by society's standards in First Century Palestine were considered to be lesser: the tax collector, the divorced woman, the woman with an internal medical condition, the lame man by the water, the blind man by the road, those stricken with leprosy, and one possessed with many demons. Among all these stories, the one that stands out is his interaction with a Samaritan woman (who the Jews would have considered lesser in no fewer than three areas — race, religion, and gender). Here we see a powerful object lesson from His life on assuming the best of others.

In a defining moment, not only for his ministry, but for world history, Jesus does more in one conversation to untangle the web of animosity and bitterness between two ethnic groups than has been done over hundreds of years. The hatred between the Jews and the Samaritans was palpable. Exchange of goods and services was permitted based upon mutual interest, but that was as far as their interactions went. There was nothing beyond mere commerce: no social, spiritual or emotional engagement.[7]   But Jesus takes it upon himself not only to travel through Samaria (most Jews would have taken the long way around), but to stop there and interact with this Samaritan woman.

Now, this woman had several strikes against her. We've established strike one: she was a Samaritan. Strike two: she was a woman. But beyond those obvious "strikes," her presence at the well at this time of day was scandalous. This almost certainly meant that she was avoiding the usual crowd of women at the well—indicating that she had done something against cultural norms and accepted morality. Yet another strike against her, especially as far as a male Jew was concerned. But Jesus changes the rules.

He begins the conversation with a basic request: a drink of water. But then he moves to something more beautiful; a conversation that hints at a future not yet present in first century Palestine. Jesus assumes the best of the woman, setting aside hundreds of years of prejudice and animosity between these two people groups. He took the situation at face value, on a level that most others wouldn't even entertain. It's just who He was and who He is.

In every interaction Jesus had with Samaritans, he did not judge them, in spite of the accompanying stigmas. Unlike the Pharisees, he embraced people from all walks of life. He would never walk across the street to avoid people. Jesus moved toward people who were different from him; not away. He wanted to get to know people, and he asked questions: What is your name? Where are your accusers? Who touched me? Who do you say that I am? These questions are only a fraction of Jesus' life and everyday engagement in relating to others. But they point to his heart for assuming the best of others, leaving speculation, negative wondering, and the rumor mill at the door. Class is in session and Jesus invites us to life's master class. What better model for leaders to follow, what better way to engage those we lead — than Jesus?

Unmasked

"People live up to – or down to – the expectations we place upon them."

Octavio:

As a child, I stuttered ho... ho... horribly. And at times, I still do. I was often sick and was perpetually skinny. I contracted pneumonia when I was eight. Did I mention I also was thoroughly, completely, and totally uncoordinated? My mother had a nickname for me: *flacosecotísico*. She said *flacosecotísico* so fast, I thought it was one word. But it was three words: Flaco. Seco. Tísico. Or in English: Skinny. Dried-Up. Sickly One. She said it so often that I thought it was my name. I didn't learn my real name until I was about 5 years old.

Nicknames are part of growing up Hispanic. My brother Cesar and sister Dora were *BooBoo* and *Fatty Girl*. I had cousins with names like *GooGoo*, *Fito* and *Cacitos*. Not even close to their given names. It's an odd form of affection I still practice.

Over time, *flacosecotísico* was dropped in favor of a new name. A new reputation. I was referred to as the troublemaker in the family. And oddly, I lived up to that name and reputation. I became convinced every problem, every pain, every pang was the result of my reputation. That is the odd, terrible power that a name, nickname, or reputation (deserved or not) has over a person: they'll live up to it. Or down to it.

The names people put on us can eventually become our identities. We end up completely internalizing these names, titles, and monikers, to the point that we *become* those identities. It's a strange, deformed sense of integrity our souls are drawn to: wanting our actions and behaviors to match our inner lives. As a result, we begin to live out the uncomplimentary identities we have internalized about ourselves.

Then it gets worse. We not only internalize the wrong, harmful name or nickname given to us by others, we not only live out that negative identity, but we take it one step further and begin to filter our entire world through the lens of that assumed identity. Like a fish in water, we have no thoughts of being wet or the limits of the bowl. What started externally with others, becomes our internal behavior, our filters. We distort our true selves and get stuck in an unholy trinity of dysfunction.

BUILDING HABITS

- Are there any nicknames or labels that others have placed on you?

- What negative or harmful assumptions have others have made about you that you've begun to internalize?

- Take a look at these false identities and begin to identify how they are not a reflection of your true self.

Once you start to change these internalized identities, and identify them as just perceptions placed on you by others, then the pendulum shifts. It's now on the other person to hold off on passing judgment until they get to know the real you. This not only frees you from the prison of others' assumptions, it enables you to begin assuming the best — of others, as well as yourself.

One of the reasons it's so difficult to assume the best is that to some extent we are all trapped inside our past hurts. But it is critical not to allow your past hurts become present emotional prison walls, holding you back from reaching your fullest redemptive potential. Just like the lens of assumed identity, past hurts can affect the way we view everything. When someone fails to meet our expectations, we run the risk of losing hope for the next relationship. Next time around, we assume the worst — we lower our expectations to avoid hurt. This may mean missing out on a great experience with a person or a community that could prove to be not only different than last time, but better than you ever imagined. When you assume the worst of others, you become reluctant to create a future alongside others. By taking on this posture, we miss out on immeasurable opportunities to learn and grow in community.

Failing to assume the best in others has another consequence: it leaves you overwhelmed with endless worst-case scenarios. You imagine all the ways the other person might do or say something that will cause you great pain. The negative outcomes you begin to work your way through can be mind-numbing to say the least. When you begin to recognize and move past your own hurts, you realize that others have been hurt, too. You realize that everyone has been injured along the way; everyone has become sensitive to all life's little bumps. When a person seems unpredictable, volatile, unstable, easily upset over the smallest things, swiftly shifting from hot to cold — it is usually because their past injuries have not healed. Don't take it personally. Step back and give them time.

Bottom line, all of us hit "bumps" in life: the car doesn't start, we get laid off, we go through a breakup, we are the butt of someone's road rage, and the list goes on. Yet if you are hurt, if you have unhealed inner wounds, these common and not so common bumps poke you on your wounds and BOOM! You explode with tears, anger, silence, depression—all signs that something is injured and unresolved in your life.

When people have chronic, repeated emotional injuries they are not able to function as they were meant to. They cannot absorb the normal bumps and bruises of life, which others may be able to handle easily. We'd never expect someone confined to a wheelchair to compete with an Olympic runner, yet we expect injured people to behave as world class athletes. You may think, "C'mon, can't they toughen up? Can't they build a bridge and get over it?" The answer is "No, they can't." Not alone. Not without a little help. You've probably been through some bumps yourself. You have no idea what someone else may be going through. Remembering your own hurts will help you leave those assumptions behind, shift your perspective, and assume the best of others.

The Genius Within

Michelangelo was just 14 years old when his talent in sculpture was noticed by the de facto ruler of Florence, Lorenzo de' Medici. Soon, young Michelangelo was adopted into the world of the powerful and influential Medici family. He was exposed to the science, art, philosophy and poetry that characterized the Medici world. He attended the Humanist academy, founded by the Medici family, where he absorbed Platonist and Neo-Platonist thought and philosophy. Before the age of 20, Michelangelo had sculpted the reliefs *Madonna of the Steps* (1490–1492) and *Battle of the Centaurs* (1491–1492). Before the age of 30, he sculpted the *Pietà* and *David*. He also painted a little: scenes from Genesis on the ceiling of the Sistine Chapel and *The Last Judgement* on the chapel's altar wall. So what?

Well, there's a lesson here. Lorenzo de' Medici took notice of this genius and drew out more than Michelangelo may have accomplished with only the guidance of his teacher, Domenico Ghirlandaio. A leader's most important job is to bring out the best in those he leads. Lorenzo de' Medici saw Michelangelo's strengths, placed him in the right environment, and connected him to the right people to help stretch his talents and equip him to succeed.

We can point to a myriad of heartfelt success stories from celebrities and successful business people who received encouragement and support from a teacher who had confidence in their potential. One person's time, care, and investment in a child can enable that child to carve out a remarkable legacy as an adult. Oprah Winfrey credits her 4th grade teacher for seeing her gifts, Bill Gates is indebted to his math and drama teachers for the extra push, and Tom Brokaw owes thanks to his elementary school teacher for encouraging him to read above grade level and use his imagination. There is something great in all of us. It's just a matter of time before we connect with our catalyst to greatness.

We've seen examples of actual leaders and influencers who used their role to bring out the best in their students—students who have made the world a better place. Now let's look at Hollywood. In the 1995 film, *Mr. Holland's Opus*, Richard Dreyfuss plays a frustrated composer who finds that his best work—his opus—was not the music he created, but the lives he changed. As a high school music teacher, Mr. Holland spent decades teaching his students to love music. Many of his students went on to become successful in different areas of life—while Mr. Holland remained in the classroom, behind the scenes of their success. Just before Mr. Holland is about to retire, a former student—now a Congressman—reminds him of the good he has done for so many with the declaration, "*We* are your opus!"

How exactly did Mr. Holland help so many teenagers become happy and amazing adults? He cared for them. He spent time with them. He passed his passion for music on to them. Assuming the best of others can also mean bringing out the best that is *already* in others. It means caring enough to perceive what is *really* inside them, rather than *your* interpretation or your idea of what their life should become. As a leader, you are not leading your team to a future; you're pulling their future out of them. As you lead and help others, consider these three Ls:

1. Learn

Learn to stay curious, my friends. Learn to ask why. Learn to hear the questions behind the questions or statements made by others. Remember, there are two mental states which are not compatible: curiosity and anger. You cannot be curious and angry in the same place and at the same time. You get to choose which you will be. Choose curiosity, and you'll assume the best of others.

2. Light

Always look for the light in people. While humans are deeply flawed, there remains a significant remnant of the image of God in all of us — regardless of who we are or what we've done. After a while, you can see some good, some light, in most people. The light may be dim, it may be covered up with layers of darkness and years of unhealthy decisions, but everyone has a bit of light. And yes: corrupt, vile and monstrous people exist in the world. It seems there is an active malevolent force working behind the scenes to further disfigure humanity's intrinsic elegance. But we don't have to participate in the further warping of human beings. Assuming the best of others is the alternative. The remedy. The treatment. When are able to recognize light in others — no matter how small or dim a spark it may be — we can assume the best. Make an intentional effort to see the light in the people you come into contact with.

3. Love

Occasionally, there's the person who isn't learning, who isn't revealing their inner light, who is a real handful. You should still assume the best of them. Why? How? Just love them. You celebrate what you can.

>You offer advice when requested.
>>You give time when needed.
>>>You give.
>>>>You give some more.
>>>>>You give a little bit more.
>>>>>>Because you love them.

And you love them because you assume the best of them. Because you assume the best of them, you see a better future for them than they see for themselves. You will never know everything these folks are currently going through, or have gone through, nor the weight of pain they carry inside themselves. But you can draw out the better future that's trapped inside. You can assume the best because you know everyone was once just a baby, a small child, a confused teenager in need of someone's care and guidance.

>*"Assuming the best of others can help untie the Gordian knot they have twisted themselves into."*

Switch gears and think about how you would deal with an old friend in the same predicament as Arthur. Arthur was a sensitive and caring poet, musician, and lyricist. Like other creative, sensitive types, without a developed healthy character, one can slide into sensuality and addictive behavior. Arthur did both.

Rejecting his spiritual heritage *and* common sense, he made one poor decision after another. He'd misspend money. He couldn't hold down a job. He failed at relationships and finally lost his dignity by turning tricks to support his heroin habit. He went from functioning adult to male hooker and heroin addict in less than a year. Not many people thought Arthur would change.

If Arthur came to you for guidance, could you assume the best of him?

What would you do?

When people are experiencing the effects of bad decisions or poor choices, whether they've done it to themselves or others have done it to them, two things get blurred: who they can be and who God is. But let's say you're not "religious." Then think of it this way; when people are experiencing the effects of bad decisions or poor choices, whether they've done it to themselves or others have done it to them, two things get forgotten:

The past is done.

There is hope for the future.

It was possible that the life Arthur was living could have gone even further down the toilet than it did. But someone spoke to him words of hope about his future. Those words of hope gave him the ability to believe that his life could change. That led to the courage to give up on a life that wasn't working and exchange it for one that would.

It takes courage to believe, and hope to see that life can be better. It's only a matter of seeing—really *seeing*—a future for people that they simply cannot see for themselves. If you can see a person's future for them—see it clearly and passionately—then you've improved the odds they will see it for themselves. When you assume the best of others, you're like an optometrist—helping others to see reality more clearly. To see what is true, not just what *feels* true. When we do not help others see what is right and true, all they can see is their brokenness, shortcomings and regrets.

According to developmental molecular biologist and research consultant Dr. John Medina's best-selling book, *Brain Rules*, we are born with a set of filters that we use to process the world, but (and this is important, so get your highlighter ready), *we create our filters by what we choose to focus on.* As a person who assumes the best of others, you give the gift of vision to those who have poor mental, emotional, or spiritual vision. Emotions and feelings are, at best, unreliable. You can trust your senses, but not your emotions. Feelings are not an indication of reality. Help others move out of their maze of emotions and provide the compass of genuine hope that somehow, one day, it will be better.

We were all born to live a life of courage and unrelenting love. Assume the best of others so they will stop letting their excuses reinforce the worst version of themselves. Sometimes, people only want to know they matter. To someone. To anyone. Someone who cares enough to stop them from—well, you name it: self injury, debt, unhealthy relationships, addiction. They want to hear someone say, "I care about you. You're not incidental. You're essential." We may never know the roads people have been on and what injuries they've sustained, but we can help them imagine the better roads that lie ahead. Help people learn to become healthy. Look for the light in each person. And love them. Even the ridiculous, hard-to-love, seemingly lost causes. They are the ones who need it most.

This kind of radical love is an act of defiance. It gives up fear and speculation in exchange for strength and truth. This demeanor moves you to be a part of a unique cohort of humanity: those who have been forgiven, and those who forgive. When you assume the best of others you constantly see others through the lens of grace. Grace is an aroma that precedes your coming and remains after you've left the company of others. It compels others to be open and honest. It is the antithesis of judgement—which gives off a smell that repels and reduces people to hide behind a mask of insecurity and disillusionment.

When you assume the best of others, people are more likely to live up to your expectations, rather than live beneath ones that were already low and ill-informed. Assuming the best of others represents humanity at its finest—a humanity that has been redeemed through the light, love, and teachings of a First Century carpenter. Jesus was well ahead of His time. He led in a way we must model and lead if we want to lead effectively and successfully.

Is there something precluding you from assuming the best of others? Is it because you've been on the receiving end of people making assumptions about you that are inaccurate? In short, self-leadership is also part of the conversation. Before you can look outward to lead others, you must begin with yourself. That includes owning up to your humanness, frailties, mistakes, sins, brokenness, bitterness, and pride. We believe these practical steps will help you flourish as you practice the habit of assuming the best of others.

BUILDING HABITS

1) Forgive Yourself: Since you are forgiven by the Creator who loves and cares for you, live your life in the light of that love and compassion. His love for you covers a multitude of sins; it forgives them. [8]

2) Forgive Others: When you've forgiven yourself and know that you have been forgiven, you are freed to extend forgiveness to others. This is a true measurement of maturity. It's also part of growing and developing as a leader.

3) Speak Up for Others: It's up to you to advocate on behalf of others—especially in their absence, especially when someone is making the worst assumptions about them. This is one of the greatest acts of honor and courage you can make as a leader. It is a weak person who stands by and allows someone's character to be demonized by the assumptions of others.

 It's worth repeating: Jesus remains the best expression of a leader who models the habit of assuming the best in others. You don't need to be a Christian or even religious to glean wisdom from His leadership. If you examine His life, as seen in the four Gospels (Matthew, Mark, Luke and John), his thoughts and attitudes toward others never come from a place of bitterness, anger, indifference, or fear—even towards his strongest antagonists and critics, the Pharisees and Sadducees. Jesus maintains a genuine concern for others, and a disposition that sees potential and promise in everyone.

In his book, *The Questions of Jesus*, John Dear affirms this truth. He writes, "He [Jesus] cultivates and holds good thoughts toward everyone.[9] He lives and breathes the truth of compassion and love and is ready to forgive and heal others because He has incarnated goodness and prayerfully nurtured good thoughts toward all people." So here's the rub: Do you want to be a better leader? Wouldn't it be great to engage and grow in relationships based on facts and not fear? It begins when you assume the best of others—something Jesus did consistently.

Dear continues by offering this admonition on assuming the best of others:

"From now on, we are to give others the benefit of the doubt, to presume the best in others, to forgive and call forth love from others, to respond instinctively with compassion toward anyone in need, to see Christ in others, to know only goodness." [10]

This type of leadership and the life of Jesus prompts the questions: Why did He do it? Why did He assume the best in others? He did it for love. In the most vulnerable and courageous way possible, He assumes the best of every person He encounters.

Judgment of others is a sign of your personal shortcomings. The more you judge, the more your insecurities are exposed.

It's tough not to judge, because our brains are predisposed to do so. Check yourself frequently. Assume the best of others because at the end of the day, you are being judged as well.

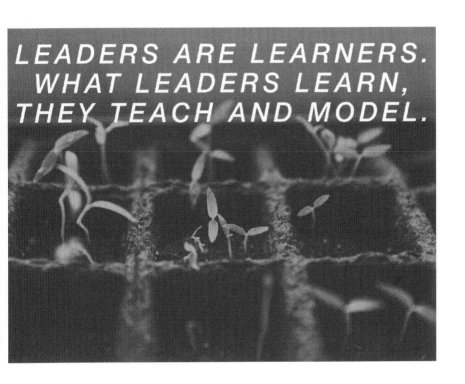

LEADERS ARE LEARNERS. WHAT LEADERS LEARN, THEY TEACH AND MODEL.

STEP 3

HABITS

BE GOOD SOIL

Are you leading from good soil so that you can embrace opportunities to learn and grow as a leader?

Our souls are gardens. And whether we like it or not, stuff will grow there—both good stuff and bad. So we need to form a habit of tending that garden, being careful about what we allow to grow. Actually, if you want a more accurate metaphor: we are less like gardens and more like the soil in a garden. Essentially, we are dirt. We need to be good dirt.

Being good soil means taking on the disposition of a learner. More specifically, it means cultivating growth in areas where you are strongest, not just trying to shore up your weak areas. This takes work. Improving in areas that you believe you have mastered takes discipline, time, and constant attention. As an influencer, you should always be in learning mode: learning even from those you disagree with.

> *"Every time you speak, you are auditioning for leadership."*
> **-James C. Humes**

There are many resources to learn from—whether you're looking for guidance on relational or leadership skills or tips for weight loss. You can even sift through history and find wisdom in the life and teachings of great stoic philosophers like Seneca and Epictetus, or the Roman emperor, Marcus Aurelius.

In the book *Meditations*, a compilation of Marcus Aurelius' thoughts, he comments on how valuable the *process* of learning is, even more so than the end result: "be satisfied with even the smallest progress, and treat the outcome of it all as unimportant."[11] And we see Seneca describe his love of learning and teaching in a letter to his friend and correspondent Lucilius. He writes, "part of joy in learning is that it puts me in a position to teach; nothing, however outstanding and however helpful, will ever give me any pleasure if the knowledge is to be for my benefit alone."[12] Not only did Seneca value learning—but it gave him the most joy when he was able to use his knowledge to lead and teach others.

We see that leaders are learners, and what leaders learn, they are willing to teach and model to those they lead. Good leaders possess a desire not to just accumulate information, but to do so for insight and transformation. They seek knowledge that can cause seismic shifts in how they think and how they lead others, knowledge that can be effective in utilizing their gifts and talents. They are willing to admit what they don't know, and they have no problem asking others who do for help. They put in the work to keep their soil healthy and ready to receive good seed that will grow.

As a leader, begin to model and practice the habit of being good soil, because it takes work. It involves consistent attention: uprooting the weeds, tilling and fertilizing the soil; it means watering and nurturing your soul to the point where it not only survives the harsh conditions life can bring, but produces growth beyond measure. Good soil does not just happen. Good soil is the most effective in nurturing growth when that soil is tended daily.

"Choose not to be harmed — and you won't feel harmed. Don't feel harmed — and you haven't been."
-Marcus Aurelius

Aurelius' words are invaluable today. There's also no shortage of contemporary wisdom we can glean. There are pop culture life coaches, wise pastors, and insightful professors...and a plethora of podcasts and TED talks and self-help books. Yet despite the wealth of available resources, people still struggle in their relational and personal growth. Why are so many people stuck in unhealthy lifestyles? Why do they consistently make destructive life-altering choices?

Easy.

Their soil needs treatment.

Their soil needs fertilizer.

Lawn Wars

Andrea is the president of her development's homeowner's association. Even though it was a volunteer position, she took her role seriously. At times, the responsibility was a bit cumbersome — managing different owners, their schedules, temperaments, and demands, often felt like a full-time job.

Late last spring, she convinced the association to authorize spending a substantial amount of resources to give an extreme makeover to their landscape. They found water-saving plants and shrubs, put in new sprinklers, and added wood chips and desert plants. For weeks, the gardeners were treating the lawn, which required a "keep off the grass" rule. The local residents disregarded the signs and the string roping off the area, not to mention the stern stares she gave over and over again for those who violated her lawn rules. She tried everything to deter neighborhood pets and their owners from tracking over the sensitive lawn, but to no avail.

After about two months of battling neighbors to keep off the grass, she tried a more direct approach. Andrea made an appeal to a few owners and told them of the extensive work involved in planning and pruning the shrubs, keeping the hedges neat and the grass manicured. She even quoted dollar figures. Still, no change. Andrea decided to forgo her continuous neighborly lawn war. She realized that as the president of the homeowner's association, it was up to her to be good soil. She was not going to let other people's stubbornness and disregard for her property, plant (no pun intended) a negative seed in her heart towards her neighbors. And the result of the Lawn War was that Andrea realized her passion for the lawn and landscape came from seeing all the work that went into the project: hours of reseeding, planting, weeding, trimming, uprooting, watering, raking, and digging. And the one key component in all of that labor? The soil.

If you want to have a great lawn—a lawn that becomes the envy of the block and the best place for pets to do their business (well, maybe you don't want that)—you have to invest in the soil. Proper nutrients (fertilizer), sunlight, watering, spacing, and even rest are all essentials for cultivating good soil. The trick for maintaining good soil is treating it for the long haul. It is an arduous process to make healthy soil, but if you choose to focus on the soil first, which may seem challenging and very unromantic, you can create a sustainable garden that will be the envy of your neighborhood. And what is true for your lawn is true for your soul. As a leader, be constantly on the lookout for growth moments, for ways you can cultivate the soil of your soul. Being good soil means cultivating your capacity to take that which is good into your heart, mind, and soul; absorbing the things that will help you grow and develop.

BUILDING HABITS

- Make this new habit personal.
- Where do you see areas of improvement in your relational growth? What do you think has contributed to this growth?
- What are the ingredients for good soil in your life? What can you take into your soul today that will help you grow and develop into good, healthy soil?

Sow, then H20

Most people are familiar with the common idiom, "you reap what you sow." It stems from scripture[13], and most literally means that whatever seeds you plant, whatever plants you cultivate — will grow. Therefore, if you sow righteousness, servanthood, or a positive attitude, you'll see those things grow and bear fruit. Conversely, if you sow sin, strife, or a negative attitude, those undesirable things will grow as well. The lesson here is: sow good seed and you will bear good fruit. Sow bad seed and destruction, and discord will take root.

"Often, we do not need more information; we need to become good soil."

Jesse is 59 years old. When he was in his twenties, he was completely unable to sustain any healthy choice for more than two years. From jobs to relationships, his character [soil] could not grow anything healthy. He read self-help books, listened to lectures, attended church, and read the Bible. Yet in the end, when under stress, he returned to violent behavior as his defense, vulgar language as his response, and pornography as his coping mechanism.

Deep inside, Jesse wanted – and tried – to be a better man. He would double-down on "seed": more books, more lectures, more sermons, more Bible study – more good, healthy information. But the result remained the same: no change, no growth, only frustration.

After one particularly awful act of violence, he reached out to a friend and disclosed all of his mess, the worst parts of his life – all of it. He no longer cared what others thought of him. In that moment, without realizing it, he pulled out the weed of pride and self-love. Unknowingly, he was allowing himself to become good soil.

Soon after, he went to see a therapist with a new willingness and ability to hear his years and years of struggle. And what Jesse heard was forgiveness: "You seem to be punishing yourself for everything you've done. But you're forgiven. Have you forgotten that?"

Jesse wept. It was not the first time he had wept. He had wept in anger. He had wept in sorrow. Yet this was the first time he wept in gratitude. He wept, knowing he had been forgiven for everything dark or awful he had ever done or thought. This time, the effect was immediate and permanent.

He spent the next 10 years learning what it meant to be human. He read more books. Everything from manners and making friends, to time management, how to dress, and how to be better at public speaking. He read about history, classical music and art. Jesse worked on his career, his relationships and his mental, emotional, and spiritual health. He became wiser and healthier than he ever imagined he could become. He was actually surprised at how easily he made progress.

But it shouldn't have been surprising at all.

After all those years of throwing good seed on bad soil, he'd finally cultivated the soil of his soul by pulling out the weeds of pride. The information he had previously taken in was able to take root and grow. He discovered he didn't need more information. To the contrary, what he had needed was to prepare his soul to take advantage of the seeds of good information. Often, we do not need more information; we need to become *good soil*. Good soil will produce so much from so little. Why? The healthier the soil, the more it produces.

We know this from gardening. The plants we want in our gardens require effort on our part to grow: breaking up soil, adding fertilizer, removing the weeds that will crowd and choke out our planted seeds. This is work. This requires effort. But growth requires something else, as well.

Water.

Water is life. Think about it. If your soul—the core of your being—is soil, then what is water?

Love.

Let's get back to Jesse. After a fast start in his thirties, his growth stalled for quite a while. His first reaction was to panic and pour on more seed. Then out of the blue, Nathaniel, who is about 20 years older than Jesse, appeared on the scene. Nathaniel is highly educated, had served in the military, and is a voracious reader. His specialty is money management, but he is particularly interested in how people thrive and grow. He has traveled the world as an international consultant on topics as varied as his reading interests. Essentially, Nathaniel is a collector: he collects, stores, classifies and gives away ideas.

More importantly, Nathaniel is also a source of water.

The water Jesse needed to jump start his growth was love and kindness. Not only did Nathaniel and Jesse become friends, but over the next few years, they traveled together internationally.

They talked for hours on planes and trains, in cabs, and over dinners which Nathaniel would make. When asked, Nathaniel would gently provide feedback and share his observations. He was Jesse's biggest cheerleader and became one of his most trusted friends. Here's what Nathaniel did: he watered the soil of Jesse's life. Do you strive to be water in the lives of those you influence? Water brings life. That life comes through love — love that we pour out into the souls of others.

Love disarms people and makes them open to healing, to better health. Love heals. Love always works and never fails to accomplish good for the person who receives it and for the person who gives it. Here's a brief look at the power of love.

Love Heals

When someone loves you in a healthy way, you also become healthier. You become stronger and more confident. Healthy love may take longer to heal one person's soul versus another — depending on the unhealthiness of the soul. In this way, love and the person being loved are similar to any illness or disease. Occasionally, the treatment takes time to have an effect — and it may initially seem worse than the disease — but it gets better. If you have ever tried to be loving to an unloving person, you know and understand what this feels like. But there's another positive effect as well. Courage. Genuine love produces courage in the healthy giver. Think about that for a moment.

Love is Courageous

Courage is the result of a deep work of love in the soul of a person. It starts with an absence of pride that manifests in humility, which is simply an accurate view of oneself. The outcome of this kind of healthy self-image is integrity: the consistent correspondence between your inner and outer life. This leads to courage: the ability to take selfless risks for the sake of others. Love makes you courageous. It takes courage to love another person and to risk being hurt or wounded in the process.

And loving Jesse was no sure thing.

Nathaniel invited Jesse into his life. He taught him, helped him, encouraged him. Dormant seeds in Jesse's soul began to grow again. But there was another result. Now Jesse had a role model to imitate. Not only did Nathaniel's love water Jesse's soul, but Nathaniel gave him another gift: an example to follow. When Jesse was in turn loving, kind, patient, and forgiving, he began to water other souls. The effect was two-fold. First: Jesse began to influence others to grow in a healthy manner. Second: Jesse continued to grow as well.

Do you want to grow?

Do you want to become a better version of yourself?

Forget getting more information.

Become good soil.

"Just because you are a CEO, don't think you have landed. You must continually increase your learning, the way you think, and the way you approach the organization."
-Indra Nooyi

Being good soil means that as a leader you are constantly on the lookout for growth moments. These moments may be new insights, approaches that are contrarian, ideas that require greater resources, new team members to strategize with, or simply time to pause, reflect, and recover. These are moments where your capacity to understand and develop as a leader is on the line. Growth moments are best realized when leaders take in new information, process it, and go on to apply it in a context and culture different from the environment where they learned it.

Implementing this habit in your life may be challenging for leaders, and high-level leaders in particular may struggle with it the most. Leaders who have a high capacity for achievement, who are pressured to succeed, are too often closed off to new information. After all, they are expected to know more, be more, and do more than those they lead. But this notion sets a leader up for ineffectiveness and failure, because growth can only take place through learning. The habit of being good soil means having the capacity to understand and appreciate what you don't know, and to be willing to adjust accordingly.

Goodie:

I grew up in the home of a single parent. My mother, who is simply an amazing woman, raised me along with my two sisters. A critical part of our upbringing as a family was our faith, and more specifically attending and participating in a local church. I am the product of a faith community, and I am thankful for the impact that community has had on my life. My faith community formed the way I view matters such as injustice, hardship, and suffering. I am aware of who I am and what my purpose is in life, largely due to my faith and understanding of who the Transcendent is, and what He has called me to be and become. Yet there is still one glaring aspect of my upbringing in a faith context that held me back rather than propelled me forward.

I grew up practicing a faith that was focused on the rules, on all the restrictions put in place to keep me from doing wrong. I grew up in a church whose unofficial name was the church of "no." There were certain places we could not go, and there were certain people we could not be associated with; there were clothes we could not wear, and music we could not listen to. As I recall, I did not hear a lot of "yes" from my faith community and its teachings. Looking back, some of these "no" moments stunted my spiritual growth. There were far too many noes and not enough statements of affirmation and encouragement. This type of spiritual culture caused me to become spiritually anemic. I was closed off to new relationships, insights, dreams, passions, and desires. I lacked vitality and passion, and was weak when it came to expressing and living out my faith. Those years of contraction, of closing off, stole many important moments from my spiritual journey. The "no" approach to faith let the soil of my soul lie untended.

Being good soil is about expansion, not contraction; it's about openness and not being closed off or indifferent. It is the antithesis of anemia. Being good soil means pursuing betterment and understanding, and being open to what others have for you — instead of afraid of negative influence. Being good soil is not lethargic when it comes to learning. It thrives on new information, on words and insights that produce growth and health in every aspect of your life as a leader.

We're Not Perfect, We're Leaders

A well-kept secret (well, maybe not so well-kept) is that leaders are insecure. Good leaders are in constant competition with their own thoughts, and those thoughts are often fueled by questions of what others think of their decisions. No matter how you try to avoid it, as a leader, bad things are going to happen — whether through your own fault or the faults of others. The trick is to learn to use the bad for good, not as a defensive mechanism, but as a tool to open up growth, new opportunities, creativity, and potential success.

There is a little known secret that gardeners know that can help change your perspective: Crap isn't always bad! Manure is one of the best forms of growth for the garden. It provides added growth and vitality for the life it is feeding, a.k.a. fertilizing. But on the surface, manure isn't pleasant. It doesn't appear to be valuable — I mean, think about where it came from!

Now, think about a team you lead or people you influence. Do any of those people seem like manure on the surface? As leaders, we sometimes want to rid the environment of the problem employee or the antagonistic team member. It may feel as though they are sabotaging all of your hard-won leadership, but take a step back and return to Step Two: Assume the Best of Others. Are these "problem" people truly toxic? Or are they just stepping on your pride a little? Maybe the reason they seem antagonistic is that their perspective is very different from your own. This practice of seeing the best in others can be hard for both the seasoned leader and the novice. But these difficult people may have a concept or process to teach you or your team; a new idea that could take root and flourish.

As you form the habit of being good soil, continue to practice the habit of assuming the best of others. These two habits go hand in hand. You can only truly be good soil, open to receiving good seed, when you assume the best of others. Assuming the best leaves you open to people and ideas you might have otherwise ignored. Seeing the best in others may be difficult, and you may still get hurt. But that pain can lead you to a place that no other incident could. Don't assume the worst because you are afraid. You are stronger and smarter than that because you know the gardener's secret: Crap isn't always bad![14]

 Jesus spoke in parables. A parable is a spiritual truth communicated in the form of a story, typically using familiar objects, situations, or contexts to bring home a point. The word "parable" comes from the Greek word *parabolee*. The first part of the word, *para*, means "beside," and the second part, *ballo*, means "to cast or throw." Thus, in the basic sense, the literal meaning of the word parable is, "to cast beside." A parable takes two ideas and sets them beside each other. It connects the unknown and the known, it bridges the sacred and the secular, and it invites its listeners to discover profound truth. Parables can help shape your spiritual and leadership journey in innumerable ways.

Jesus tells a parable about a farmer spreading seed. We see the farmer going out to plant seed, but some of the seed fails to take root in the soil. Some landed along the pathway, where feet trampled it. Some seeds fell on rock, where it could not take root. Other seeds fell among thorns and although the seed began to grow, the plants were choked out before they could reach maturity. Still, other seeds fell on good soil, and the result was a crop one hundred times more than what was sown.[15]

In this passage, Jesus, tells his listeners to pay attention and receive his message. If you want to be successful, which "results in a crop one hundred times more than what was sown," give care to where you place your seed. The various places where the seed falls represent the human soul, and the varying degrees of responsiveness to the word of God. If the soil is unresponsive, the seed will not take root. This is a leadership lesson on multiple levels. Not only must we be good soil, we must plant seeds in good soil. You may spread your great ideas far and wide, but if your team is not in line with your vision, or they don't trust you, the seeds of your great idea will not take root, and will never come to fruition. You must cultivate the soil before your seeds can take root.

Jesus was making it simple for us. Good soil produces the most fruit. If you are intentionally operating with good soil as a leader, and are effective in creating and fertilizing good soil amongst your team, the results will be successful. Remember, Jesus was talking to a group of people that was very familiar with the language of agriculture. They were farmers, and they understood how detrimental it was to have no crop, or very little crop — and how life-changing it was to have a crop produce one hundred times more than was planted.

This parable speaks to an overall principle that will make influencers become better leaders. If something is true, if something is of value — be open to it taking root in your life. When opportunities are presented, don't be indifferent or closed off (like the bad soil in the parable). When your soul is made up of good soil, when you practice the habits of having fun and assuming the best of others, you will be open to new seed taking root in your life. You will be more willing to learn advanced concepts, work with diverse people, and embrace challenges. Being open to learning — being good soil — will yield a harvest in immeasurable ways: faith, wisdom, and both emotional and physical health.

The Right Season

Getting the soil just right takes time. Soil, like the human heart, is temperamental. There are times and seasons for tilling and sifting the soil. What is true for dirt is true for the human soul, mind, and spirit. It is important to recognize those seasons when you are keenly aware of learning moments, when you are ready to fully engage the highest levels of learning and understanding. However, you should also recognize those times when you are not in a mode of receiving.

Those who desire to lead others at the highest levels must be aware when this *engagement gap* occurs. If you are aware of this gap, you can make adjustments in order to continue to be effective. This temporary gap can allow you to delegate a higher level of responsibility to a qualified team leader. If you know you will be unable to receive all that an opportunity has for you, offer it to a team member. Have them report back to you what they gleaned from the discussion. Sometimes, you may just need a break. We can only take in so much before we need time to process what we've learned. Asking for a break, stepping away for a moment (or longer, as needed) will allow you to regroup and process, and be able to re-engage and be present when you step back in. Identifying these gap moments, and adjusting accordingly, will keep you from feeling overwhelmed, and will allow the time you need for the seed you have received to take root.

Being good soil is not only about what you take in, but also about what you give out. Soil starts as dirt, but becomes good soil by being enriched by nutrients, fertilizer, water and sunlight. Soil is filled with good things so that it can give back life to plants and flowers. Good soil is the opposite of selfish. It is an interdependent relationship where one or more parties are dependent upon the other for survival. Good soil takes in the good in order to enrich itself – but also to pass that enrichment on to others. Great leaders are not only learners; they are life-givers.

 If you think you know everything, you probably know nothing. The sooner you activate your mindset to regularly seek personal growth and development, and embark upon nurturing others, joy and fulfillment will follow. Be good soil, not just manure!

STEP 4

HAB**I**TS

INSIST UPON EXCELLENCE

When you insist upon excellence, how do you measure progress?

> *"We are what we repeatedly do. Excellence, then,*
> *is not an act but a habit."*
> **-Will Durant**

This is a great quote that has often been credited to Aristotle, but in fact, Will Durant said it. Who? Will Durant. He's the author of *The Story of Philosophy: The Lives and Opinions of the World's Greatest Philosophers.* Durant was summing up a few of Aristotle's thoughts in Part VII of his book, dealing with "Ethics and the Nature of Happiness." We need to be reminded that excellence is not a one-off effort, a chance event, only for world-class performers. Excellence is the result of everything we've done until now. Demean, distort, or discount your character, and no matter how talented you are, you will not be able to sustain excellence.

Insisting upon excellence at its core is about two things: presentation and essence. The former has to do with how something appears. The latter has to do with who you are at your core, and your heart's desire as a leader. You can never go wrong in a heartfelt pursuit of both.

Shawn had started a couple of non-profits, an online magazine and was the executive producer of several concerts and a public access TV show. He was no stranger to hard work—he did all of this while working full time as a Business Account Executive (i.e. fancy salesperson). There were two questions he often asked both himself and his team: *How was excellence achieved? Why did this succeed?* If no one in the room could answer those two questions, he knew their results were not necessarily based on skill or talent. They'd just gotten lucky. If you don't know *how* you succeeded, you may hit excellence again by accident, but your random luck will eventually run its course. Achieving excellence must be *intentional.*

You may be like Shawn—juggling many balls in the air and living with various sets of tension. When under stress, multi-taskers like Shawn make quick decisions that rarely result in solutions, decisions that are just a quick fix until the next time they have to deal with the problem. And there will be a next time. The flip side of quick decisions made under stress is procrastination. These two tendencies seem at odds with each other—but they often go hand in hand. Multi-taskers are great at procrastination, waiting till the last minute for an amazing idea or strategy to surface and launch the project into the stratosphere of excellence. And just like knee-jerk decisions, this strategy rarely works.

Are there any similarities between you and Shawn?

What do you do well?

How do you do what you do well—when do you do your best work?

Think about the time of day, location, or circumstance, in which you are the most productive. Knowing your stride is important and can help you focus on other things until you have to "turn on." Many people prefer early mornings for tackling things they dislike or tasks that require concentration. Early mornings will likely bring fewer distractions to your workflow, and by 10:00 a.m., you will find that you've completed at least one or two important things on your "to-do" list. Once these are accomplished, you are fueled to tackle the rest of your day—or even the next day's list.

Don't fall into the trap of creating unrealistic "to-do" lists that leave you feeling stressed and unproductive. Negative emotions will continue to weigh you down. Not only will excellence be out of your reach, it will not even be on your radar.

Octavio:

I'm a classic late bloomer. I didn't speak well past the norm for children. I was even slow in learning to walk. I entered university for the first time at the age of 52. Four years later, I graduated with a degree in analytical philosophy and two minors: theology and art. I learned it's one thing to read about philosophy. It is quite another to read philosophy. Original source material is tough going at times, especially at night, after a long day, when you're tired and hungry; especially when you have not completed your weekly 20 page reading assignment and accompanying 3-5 page paper. And that was one class. Did I mention that at the time, I was also the director of a growing non-profit?

Out of necessity, I had to quickly learn when and how I do my best work. I discovered that my creative muse will show up in the cold, dark, early morning hours of a coffee shop. After a bacon and egg breakfast, my best time for creative thinking or work is from 4:00-9:00 a.m. Then I'll take a 1-2 hour break for some emails or phone calls, and updating my calendar. After a light lunch, I have an early afternoon burst of critical, analytical thinking and writing. By 4:00 in the afternoon, I'm useless for my best work, so I take in information: read books, watch documentaries, movies, or meet someone for conversation. For other people, other times may be better for different types of work, but for me to insist on excellence, I need to (as much as possible) stick to this schedule.

Now, insisting upon excellence does not mean always being "on" and "making an impact." It leaves room for grace—an amazing grace that is extended not only to yourself as a leader, but is also freely given to those you lead. All too often, leaders are in denial of their developmental needs and waste years consciously doing things that don't work. After striking out countless times with procrastination and juggling several projects, Shawn was beginning to feel the weight of all his responsibilities. So he asked a friend for some advice. This friend was busy: married with kids, led a large team, kept up a heavy speaking schedule, wrote books, led meetings and retreats, met with people frequently — everyone wanted some of his time. So Shawn asked him: "How do you do it all?" His answer was surprising: you have to do things with no redemptive value.

And yet his answer made all kinds of sense. We all need to unplug and turn off to recharge at times. The work will still be there when we plug back in. But by recharging, we come back to work with a different perspective and are able to accomplish more. Following a regular schedule of downtime and feeding yourself with good healthy input is a sign of maturity — and a strategy for excellence. If you're going to insist on excellence, make sure you have something to offer — mentally, emotionally, spiritually. For that, you need to recharge, refuel, recreate, and rest.

Excellence isn't timeless.

Excellence must be maintained.

Excellence has an expiration date.

BUILDING HABITS

- What are some of your best creative, productive moments?

- When and where do you do your best work?

- What do you need most in order to recharge?

If you're not sure of the answers to these questions, try this:

- At the end of the day, write down a summary of what happened that day: What did you think? When did you feel most yourself? What were you doing when you experienced an "aha" moment?

- Take note of the time of day and the type of environment that are most conducive to your work. Plan your work in order to leverage these times and spaces. If necessary, go to bed sooner, get up earlier, cut out mind numbing activities like video viewing, video gaming or social media.

- Pay attention to the activities that help you relax and refuel. Then give yourself permission to indulge in those activities, without feeling guilty about not being productive.

"If you are going to achieve excellence in big things,
you develop the habit in little matters. Excellence
is not an exception, it is a prevailing attitude."
-Colin Powell

One of the most interesting things about Bible stories are the details, specifically the ones that are left out. In Chapter One, we looked at the story of Jesus turning water into wine — but we're going to take another look here. When reading this story, there are some "missing details" you might have wondered about:

1. Why were Jesus and his family invited?
2. Who was the couple? Were they family? Friends?
3. Would the couple look back and recall Jesus had attended?
4. If they did, what would they tell their kids about Jesus?
5. Did the couple become followers of the early Jesus movement?

But another question we think about is the wine: what was that wine like?

Octavio:

I'm not big on wine. I don't care for dry wines, and sweet wines give me headaches. But one day, I went to lunch at a local eatery and chatted with Kyle, the owner. We began to talk about different beers and wine. Excitedly, he said, *"Oh, pastor, you've got to taste this."* He poured a quarter-glass of red wine and handed it to me. I was not excited, but I put on my game face, thanked him, and took a sip.

Wow.

It was incredible. Like drinking the laughter of children. It was excellent. I remember thinking: *"So THIS is how wine is supposed to taste."*

So, what was that water-turned-into-wine like? It was excellent.

"Everyone brings out the choice wine first and then the cheaper wine after the guests have had too much to drink; but you have saved the best till now." – John 2

Of course it was the best. Of course. That's what God would do. He would insist on excellence.

And so we, as His followers ought to follow His lead. Do your best. Be known for insisting on excellence.

Say Goodbye to Freedom

Insisting upon excellence is a quid pro quo exchange. It's a trade-off—if you insist on excellence, you will have to give up some of your freedom. If your freedom is more important, then you're only kidding yourself when you say excellence is your priority. Here are three simple (but not easy) rules to intentionally insist on excellence. But if followed, these rules will require the surrender of some of your personal freedoms.

• *Do what's right.* If you have to talk yourself into taking an action, or if you hope no one ever discovers what you're doing, STOP. You're violating your conscience which is never right or safe.

• *Do everything to the best of your ability.* Relationships: personal and public. Professional life. Diet, fun, appearance. Everything.

• *Show people you care.* This does not mean you'll always make life easy for everyone. Nor does this mean you'll always say "Yes" to every request. However, it does mean you'll take time to learn about what you can do to show those around you that they are valued and cared for.

Now imagine an organization, group, or family where everyone did these three things for each other. Start with you.

Teach others to do the same and you'll always have a thriving organization where people thrive—and that type of organization will produce excellence.

Everyone is Watching

Remember, what you allow is the culture you create. You can hang motivational posters in the hallways. You can talk about your personal and professional values. You can say all the right things at all the right times. Yet people will believe what they see and experience, regardless of your words. Here are three questions people often ask about their leaders. How would the members of your family, team, or staff answer them?

1. *Can I trust you?*
2. *Do you care about me?*
3. *Are you committed to excellence?*

The habit of insisting upon excellence is working to be the best version of yourself. It is important not to confuse excellence with perfection. Sadly, most young MBA interns have had to learn this difference the harsh way. These new fresh-faced university grads bound into their internships focused on one thing: proving their excellence at the job. They appear to be driven work-horses, with perfectionist loyalty to their work, yet have a general air of unapproachability. They often refuse to ask for help because in their minds, perfection is not a team effort. These interns do everything they can to prove their perfection while hiding their imperfections. They are in search of perfection, believing it will lead to their dream career.

And to their dismay, what their employers or future employers want is not perfection. Employers are looking for trust. Harvard social psychologist Amy Cuddy found some staggering truths in her research in this area.[16] She boiled it down to two questions people ask when they size you up: i) Whether you will be a good leader or ii) whether you will be good at your job.

People are looking for two critical answers about your leadership: Can I trust this person? Can I respect this person? Cuddy and her colleagues translated those two questions into two descriptives: warmth and competence. Shockingly, her research found that competence was secondary to warmth or trust. Employers want to know if a potential employee is trustworthy. Trustworthiness was demonstrated by openness, asking for help, building social relationships, and engaging in honest dialogue with colleagues.

Employers don't care so much that you can do the job or even do it superbly. They are more concerned with your character — whether you'll be deceitful, use the organization for your benefit, or fail to uphold its values. Cuddy believes that this mindset goes back to cavemen days. During that time, if a stranger came into your territory, your main concern was whether he was going to kill you or take all of your possessions. Not whether he could make a fire or kill that night's dinner.

We revert back to this mindset every day in both corporate and casual settings. We've noted that the top question for employees is whether they can trust their leaders. Now research has demonstrated that employers have the same question in mind when hiring you. Even if you are more qualified than other candidates, if your employer can't trust you, someone else will get the job.

How often do we as leaders expect perfection of ourselves or the people in our spheres of influence? What is the goal: perfection or being your best self?

Done Too Well

Goodie:

Have you ever been accused of being too good or too excellent? Is there such a thing? For most of my life, I struggled with math and science in school. And in seventh grade, I knew I had to work extra hard when the science project came around. It was a big deal and accounted for half of the semester's overall grade—and Ms. Jones was known to be a tough grader.

Every student was required to conduct a scientific experiment that included a class demonstration, visuals, a written report and a brief explanation of the importance of your scientific project to society. I chose to do my project on volcanic explosions and the impact they have on our climate and geography. I even got dry ice from Baskin-Robbins to make a "lava" eruption happen in front of the class.

My presentation went great. My classmates were wowed by the fake smoke and lava oozing down the sides of the handmade mountain of clay. My verbal presentation was top notch. A few days later, the reports were handed back, and mine had a note from Ms. Jones saying, "See me for your grade."

I arrived at her desk shortly after school, and in no uncertain terms she accused me of having someone else do my project. She said the classroom presentation was impressive, but not consistent with my abilities and previous work. She was particularly critical of the written report—saying it was not my original work. She summed up her accusations by saying that the work itself was too excellent to be my own.

Eventually, my mom was called in for a conference. When Ms. Jones pulled our the written report, my mom vouched for me, arguing fervently that the work was all mine. The point of contention was this: Ms. Jones noted that the work presented in the formal written report was not in my handwriting. This was factually indisputable. The written report was in all blue ink and in beautiful cursive writing.

Even today, I still have bad penmanship. Since I knew 50% of my grade was at stake, I'd written the report out in pencil and enlisted my mother to copy it over, word-for-word. It was my mom's handwriting—that was true. But these were my words and my thoughts. Every detail was my original work—from the report to the presentation to the in-class lava explosion. My goal was excellence—which was why I enlisted my mother as my personal scribe.

Eventually, Ms. Jones relented and gave me a "fair grade" of a B. She maintained a great deal of suspicion about me and my efforts for the rest of the semester. And her words have remained with me for over thirty-five years: "This is too excellent. It is done too well to be from you."

In my pursuit of excellence, I failed to realize that my mom's handwriting took away from my credibility. My poor penmanship didn't diminish the quality of my research, my writing, or my presentation. But my attempt to cover up my weakness of lousy handwriting opened up questions about my project's authenticity.

BUILDING HABITS

- Have you ever been in Goodie's situation— of being "too good" in your work?

- Have you ever pursued excellence so hard that you went out of your way to cover over minor imperfections?

- Are you too hard on yourself?

Excellence has less to do with perfection, and more to do with being the best version of yourself. Excellence is not a mandate that demands purity and errorless work from yourself or others. Instead, it is an attitude that says as a leader, you will bring to bear all your skills, talents, and gifts, in order to achieve a mission or a goal. Insisting upon excellence thrives on the process that it takes to achieve excellence.

Often we place people in positions of responsibility only when we think they are ready. We expect perfection before responsibility. But when we do this, we forfeit the process that prepares a person for excellence, and the learning experience that comes from growing and developing over time. Insisting upon excellence is not about the end product, or about excelling at any cost. It's not about dotting every I and crossing every T. It is more concerned with you seriously taking on the role and responsibility of leadership, and acting accordingly.

Whatever bar for success you've established as a leader, there is another level. Regardless of the distance you've traveled or what heights you've climbed, there is more to master. Insisting upon excellence recognizes these truths. Yet, there is also a recognition that achieving such heights and successes does not come from a win-at-all costs mentality. Insisting upon excellence is not a burden you place upon yourself or on others. Instead, it's celebrating and encouraging others to live up to their fullest redemptive potential, and expecting nothing less from yourself and those you lead.

Insisting upon excellence moves to the rhythm of grace. It is devoid of judgement towards yourself — or others — when you fail. This is not to say that you don't have high expectations or set goals that will stretch people. Your teams still need to be challenged beyond what they may have known or experienced in the past. As a leader, you've been granted permission to influence and lead the most valued commodity on the planet: people. People deserve your best leadership. They deserve your best self. Practically speaking, everything should be done in a way that celebrates this truth.

Take a Break or Be Broken

As a leader, staying mentally and physically fit for the challenges that come with the day is critical. Working long hours or every day of the week can be taxing on your mind and body. Most people with a strong work ethic learn this the hard way.

In his first year of starting a second non-profit, Glenn's schedule was grueling. He was working full time managing millions of dollars of revenue—revenue he was expected to increase. The non-profit was growing faster than he had imagined, and he was responding to over a hundred emails each day. That same year he took over 120 speaking engagements. He led meetings, attended meetings, attempted to maintain some semblance of a social and family life. Glenn often joked, "I'll sleep when I'm dead."

Unfortunately, like the proverbial frog in the slow pot of boiling water, he didn't realize the dangerous waters he had been treading. He began to self-anesthetize to cope. After quitting ten years earlier, he started smoking again. Within two weeks, he was a pack-a-day Marlboro 72's smoker. He started drinking. At first, just one whiskey, then two. But both before noon. Then a few beers at night to wind himself down. Since Glenn never took a break from work, the work began to break him.

One day, while driving to see an important client, he lost control of his bladder. He was was completely unaware of it until that unfathomable moment when he "felt" it. The silver lining? Glenn was wearing a dark suit. He went to his meeting. It was similar to doing a good job at some corporations: you get a warm feeling but no one really notices.

It was then he finally realized he needed a break. He swallowed his pride and told his supervisors he needed medical leave. He took six weeks off, traveled to India with friends, and while there, ate a vegetarian diet to detox. He healed physically, mentally and spiritually. Learn from Glenn's mistakes: Yes, it is great to insist upon excellence, but take time off to recharge, refuel, recreate, and rest. And not just six weeks of medical leave after you've broken. Build rest into your routine.

You'll prolong your usefulness.

You'll save yourself from embarrassment.

And you'll save on your dry cleaning bills.

BUILDING HABITS

- How many hours a week are you "working"? 60? 80? More?
- How do you recharge? When do you recharge?
- Can you imagine running at your current pace for the next few years?

If you're working too many hours a week without regularly recharging, or if you can't imagine keeping up the same pace for the next few years, try this:

• Spend 1-2 hours next week, examining which responsibilities you can let go of, and let go of them. Ask someone to take a look at your work load to see what can be delegated or set aside for now.

• Do what makes you happy. Go see a movie, take a walk, read a book — do something to help you recharge.

• Consider if the work you're doing is worth doing. If it is, get healthy and stay healthy: physically, mentally and spiritually. Remember: it's a marathon, not a sprint.

Excellence is not a relative term. It is an intentional practice. When you insist upon excellence, you reject mediocrity and explore avenues for continuous improvement in every area of your life. Go strong or don't go at all!

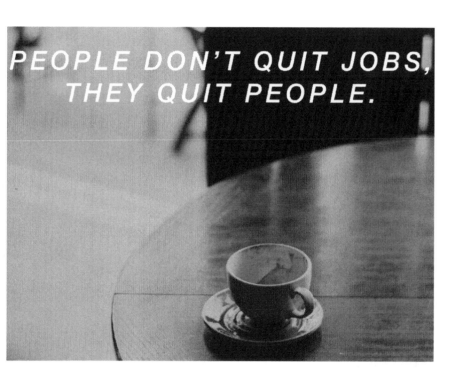

PEOPLE DON'T QUIT JOBS,
THEY QUIT PEOPLE.

STEP 5
HABITS

TREAT OTHERS AS SACRED

How do you treat people who need your help?

Important is one thing.

Sacred is another thing.

Important is: *significant, consequential, momentous, critical, crucial, vital, pivotal, urgent, historic; serious, grave, weighty, material, or impactful.*

Sacred is: *holy.*

Have you ever considered the difference between an old, faded, wrinkled, torn-and-taped-up $50 bill and one that's crisp, new, and fresh-off-the-press? Absolutely nothing. They both have the same value. No matter how damaged, they both give the bearer $50 worth of purchasing power. The same is true for a piece of art. If a priceless artwork is discovered, even if it's damaged or buried under layers of dirt and grime, it is still priceless. Careful attention is given to restore it to its former state. Yet with people—specifically with damaged people—we do the opposite, and discard them. How much more valuable is a person than a $50 bill, or even a priceless work of art! A key habit of a leader is seeing the intrinsic worth and value of human beings. And where that habit starts is treating others — and their needs — as sacred.

The essence of treating people as sacred is being present when leading others, being fully alive and aware in the moment. Often, leaders struggle to shift the focus from themselves to those they lead. But taking an interest in the lives of others goes far in building relational capital with your team. Those you lead need to know that you care, and that their needs matter to you. Sometimes those needs aren't immediately apparent — they require investigation, reflection, asking the right questions. Understanding those needs requires relationship, and time. But sometimes needs are as simple as encouragement, affirmation, or simply taking an interest in the lives of those you lead. Even small gestures quickly add up to big things. And big things are what move and motivate people to achieve a mission or task greater than themselves.

Who are you inviting to be a part of the mission?

What are their hopes, dreams, fears, and passions?

What are you doing to meet their needs and nurture them in relationship to you as a leader?

"Employees who believe that management is concerned about them as a whole person — not just an employee — are more productive, more satisfied, more fulfilled. Satisfied employees mean satisfied customers, which leads to profitability."
-Anne M. Mulcahy

Often it takes just one simple question to get your teams to perform better. Asking "How are you feeling?" can make a person's day. In fact, it might be the smartest thing you do in your day. Tony Schwartz, president and CEO of the Energy Project shared some of his learning and insight with *Business Insider* magazine on what made his team perform better.[17] He found that one of the simplest things he could do was to create safe communication environments within his teams, which led to connection, and produced better overall performance. This wasn't a time for a counseling session to find out why someone felt a particular way, but a simple information-gathering moment about work and non-work related events.

> *"When you really listen to another person from their point of view and reflect back to them that understanding, it's like giving them emotional oxygen."*
> **-Jim Rohn**

What was the larger dynamic happening at work beyond safe communication and team connection? It conveyed to the team members that their work roles, office environment and personal lives mattered. To most, this may seem too simple and not a good business strategy, but Schwartz would strongly disagree. Just imagine the impact to your team if you know first-hand that a colleague is dealing with a family crisis or a milestone that she is anxious about. You now have greater emotional intelligence in how to approach her, and know better how to allow for her needs within the context of your team. This simple task not only communicates the belief that others' needs will be treated as sacred, it can also help you and your team to be more effective in your work and in managing your time and resources. Treating people's needs as sacred isn't just a trite leadership point, it is an efficient and effective way of exceeding your goals.

Undivided Attention

People don't quit jobs; they quit people. A colleague recently shared his frustration about his boss of five years. Brad spoke in depth about why he was becoming increasingly disappointed. What was a seemingly good relationship had gone south. The pay was good, and the work itself was not laborious or mundane. In fact, Brad not only loved what he did, he was the best in the company — head and shoulders above his peers.

He described a recent interaction he had with his boss that

summed up their relationship and his overall disillusionment in working for the company. "I walked into my boss' office; he was expecting me and this was my moment to put these past few months of discontent all out on the table," Brad said. "But as I weighed in on my concerns about our relationship and my role in the company's success, my boss never looked up. Not once. I wanted to quit my job right on the spot."

Throughout their meeting, Brad's boss continued to multi-task—checking emails and making notes unrelated to their conversation. When Brad saw his boss' lack of interest, lack of respect, and failure to hear his needs, his mind was made up. He diverted the conversation to inconsequential chit chat, and quickly ended the meeting. Brad walked out of his boss' office sad, and most of all, feeling unheard and unsupported.

Can you empathize with Brad?

Or have you been guilty of multi-tasking when someone is speaking with you?

How often have you failed to give someone your undivided attention?

When was the last time you made a person feel as though they were the most important person in the room?

Treating the needs of others is seeing past yourself: It's looking up, and realizing that the person standing in front of you is worthy of your full and undivided attention. Treating the needs of others as sacred is coming to grips with the fact that the world does not revolve around you as a leader—rather, it's just the opposite. It means you take selfless risks for the good of others, earnestly seeking to understand the best ways you can serve those you lead. It's time for us as leaders to recognize that the room is so much bigger than us.

"The essence of leadership is servanthood."

No person in human history modeled the habit of treating others as sacred more than Jesus. In his book, *The Politics of Jesus,*

Obery Hendricks offers a resoundingly beautiful understanding of this idea. The sum of Hendricks' assertion is this: there is one consistent thread that runs through all Jesus' interactions with people: he treated their needs as holy. Doing this communicates the belief that responding to others' needs is an act of reverence. It means to hold not only the person in high regard, but to hold their needs, concerns, fears, dreams, and hopes in high regard as well. We are indebted to Hendricks for his academic excellence, yet the world is immeasurably more beautiful and forever changed because of the life and teachings of Jesus, and how he modeled the habit of treating others as sacred.

Ally from the Podium

For those of you who are professors, the highest compliment you could ever receive from a student is not excitement over fair grading practices, celebratory accolades about your lectures, or feedback about your charming personality. Instead, it's the compliment from a student who stated that you treated his needs as sacred; that you saw the needs of others, and addressed those needs with great care and compassion. As challenges come during the course of a semester and students are pressed on so many levels, they will look for someone to allay their fears and disillusionment. Students will question their academic ability, agonize over social insecurities, and may also question their faith. And in the midst of those questions, students will often look to professors for help and guidance.

Meeting with a student to discuss an assignment, offer extra help, or provide insight on a subject discussed in class can have a profound impact for years to come. Especially if you continue to make time for that student after he's completed your class. Think about those professors who gave you their undivided attention, rooted for your success, and found ways to engage your learning process outside of the classroom and into the school of life. Students will gravitate towards and be forever grateful to professors who treated their needs as sacred, and made them feel significant and valued.

Think about that summation for a moment. What a great tribute from a student about a teacher – or from a follower to a leader. How can you measure those words when you hear them as a leader coming from people who follow you? Treating the needs of others as sacred does not mean people agree with every decision you make as a leader. Nor does it mean you are free of mistakes, or that you are no longer in need of growth and development. Instead, treating the needs of others as sacred demonstrates that you value others not simply for what they do, but for who they are – human beings created in the image of God.

 Scripture shows us that Jesus served his disciples by washing their feet, and then encouraged them to also serve one another.[18] Not only did Jesus treat the needs of others as holy on numerous occasions, but all of his acts stemmed from love – *agape* love, which is the highest form of love. *Agape* is a self-sacrificing love, the love that God has for all of his children. It is because of God's love for us that he gave us his only Son, Jesus.[19] Love, service, and humility go hand-in-hand. They are three characteristics that connect us to our purpose on Earth. If you make a habit of doing things not out of selfish ambition, but with humility, and put the needs of others first, you will be like-minded with Christ.[20] Who better to be compared to?

Safe Encounters

Adriana was living with friends when she was still in high school. Her mom and stepdad never reached out to look for her. They didn't seem to care where she was, or who she was with. When she was invited by a pastor and his wife to stay in a spare bedroom, she immediately took the offer. Adriana thrived in this home and stayed with them for just under two years. She went on to complete both her undergraduate and graduate degrees, and today is a professor at a well-known college.

Do you think Adriana would have become successful without the invitation to live in a stable home? Maybe. Maybe not. That's not the point. The point is to treat the needs of others as sacred — you never know who they were meant to become, or who they could become, if given the support they need.

Octavio:

Not long ago, I attended my 40th high school reunion. That's where I came across Oscar. I sat near the photo booth, watching many of my former classmates stop by to take pictures. One of those classmates was Oscar. I didn't remember him until he began to tell me an incredible story.

I used to volunteer at a local church in Huntington Park. One night during a service, I happened, to step outside. Oscar was there. He didn't come to attend the service. He came to set the place on fire. He really came to burn the building down.

We barely knew each other then. We were surprised to see each other that night. I was further surprised to hear why he was there. He was angry and bitter over a personal issue with someone inside the church, and he came to get revenge. With fire. He planned to burn down his friend. And everyone else. And the church on top of that. But then he ran into me.

Oscar told me what he intended to do and why. And I told him, "No." I cared about that silly old church and all the people inside of it. I can recall thinking what a coward I would be if I did nothing. I told him: "Those people matter. That building matters. And *you* matter. Don't do it."

Oscar walked away.

I never told anyone about that night. I don't think I'd thought about it since that night. Decades later, we stood face-to-face again. He hugged me and thanked me for speaking to him so many years ago. He told me I'd saved him from making the biggest mistake of his life. He's now a happily married man, a father, and a grandfather. He went on to have a successful career. He's had a good life full of good work, and is now retired. All of that could have gone up in smoke—his life and mine—if I hadn't stopped him from setting fire to an old church full of people. Before I knew how to articulate it, I treated the lives of others as sacred—that church full of people, but also Oscar himself. And it made all the difference. That's something that we as leaders must never forget.

Wellness to Go

Generally, most leaders, pastors, politicians, and CEOs start off on the right foot. They wish to help, serve, lead or make a profit by filling a need—creating something people need or want. One person with a vision and the ability to communicate that vision can be powerful. All great movements start this way.

The visionary draws a group of people around her, persuades a group of investors to trust her. Teams are chosen. Meetings are held. Plans are drawn up and executed. Soft and hard launch target dates are set. Then it happens: the product is shipped, the service is held, a bill is passed. Cheers all around.

That's when it can begin to go off the rails. The organization, the brand, the party, the company, or worse—the leaders themselves—become more important than the people they wanted to serve. It happens over and over. And when it happens, the consequences seep into the organization itself. What people do becomes more important than the people who do it.

So what do you do if a key person loses focus? We immediately start asking questions:

How do we keep him going?

Who can replace him?

We need him to do ____!

The answer?

We don't.

Who knows?

We don't.

People are more important than what they do. People often learn in the thick of things: a crisis, a loss, a transition or a big public failure. It's usually a naked moment and they need a curtain of charity to cover their nakedness. Remember, we learn in failure and loss—if we can process the event accurately to recognize the next step or call for help. It's a skill. It's a need. So when someone close to you fails, be the first to lend your hand and help them up. Protect their reputation. Allow them a pause to get well again. This is not the time for "I told you so" or that great lesson which you were "waiting for the right moment to share." It's the time to sit with them, walk with them, and listen to them. Offer feedback only when asked. If done correctly, you'll move them from harm to health. Learn to say kind, specific words of hope before a criticism. Speak the truth, but lead with love.

When you compliment, say *you*.

When you critique, say *we*.

And when you love, love hard.

BUILDING HABITS

- With everyone you meet, you're nudging them a little closer to a heaven or a hell. How are you doing in this area?
- How do people experience you?
- What marks are you leaving on people?

If there ever was a misunderstood, slandered person, it's Thomas. Did this guy get a lousy deal or what? He will forever be known as Doubting Thomas. Even if you've never stepped into a church in your life, you probably know the story of Doubting Thomas.

But let's say you have no idea who this Thomas guy is ... what did he do? Or didn't do? What did he doubt? Well, he doubted Jesus (for the record, all of us have). But specifically: he doubted Jesus had physically resurrected from the dead, was alive again, and had spoken to his 10 friends (Judas had, well... already left the group).

Here's how it happened. First, some context. Jesus gathered 12 guys to be his first class of students: followers, who are more commonly known as disciples. They were quite a mixed bag: an accountant type who collaborated with the occupying enemy, a terrorist, a teenager, a seminary student, several small business owners. All Jewish. All male. For almost three years, Jesus as Rabbi poured his life into these men. And the goal of a rabbi's follower was not only to know what the rabbi knew, but to become who the rabbi was.

In those three years—if the stories are true, and there are significant, historical, sufficient reasons to believe they are—those men became deeply devoted to their rabbi. They respected and loved him. But when it really mattered, they abandoned their beloved rabbi. They were too afraid to be associated with him for fear they would have to die for him. Out of fear, Jesus' closest friend, Peter—who hours earlier claimed he would die for him—denied knowing him. All of them were on some level, doubters.

We're not told why Thomas was not present when Jesus first appeared to the remaining 10 disciples. But maybe—Thomas' heart was broken. Torn out, stomped on, crushed. You see, the last thing Thomas had heard about his beloved rabbi was that he'd been arrested, tried for treason (a capital offense), and found guilty. Thomas knew that Jesus was about to join the ranks of crucified upstarts, executed publicly as a warning to others that that type of behavior was not welcomed or appreciated. And crucifixion was a brutal, slow, humiliating execution. Our word, excruciating comes from the Latin, "out of the cross" to describe the unique, exquisite pain from a crucifixion.

Back to Thomas' whereabouts. It is a safe guess that he was alone with his broken heart. When your world is annihilated, when all hope is taken away, when the light of your life is extinguished, when love dies... you tend to want to be alone. So when all his buddies tell him Jesus is alive, it was understandable not to believe them. Dead men don't get up and live again. He wasn't going to have his heart broken again, his hopes dashed. He did not want to believe them—not without absolute proof. It was likely through tears when he uttered those famous words, "*Unless I see the nail marks in his hands and put my finger where the nails were, and put my hand into his side, I will not believe.*" So Jesus treated

Thomas' needs as holy. He obliged him. The God of the Universe treated the needs of one of His creatures as sacred. Jesus showed up, and said to Thomas: "Touch and see." [21]

While many people know Thomas doubted Jesus' resurrection, what many people do not know is what Thomas did with the rest of his life. Tradition tells us that he travelled outside the Roman Empire, preaching along the way as far as Tamil Nadu and Kerala in present-day India. He is the founder of a Christian sect known as the Saint Thomas Christians or Nasranis. Even today, *Thoma* is one of the most popular names among the Nasranis. And what did Thomas preach? Jesus is alive!

People, Not Projects

The more talented a person is, the more difficult it is to remember that people are not projects. We are not machines — we are more elegant. We are designed, not manufactured. And unlike machines, you can't push a button or pull a lever and make everything work again. There isn't anyone with a quick reboot switch.

If you're in charge of others, latch on to three things:

1. *get.*
2. *self.*
3. *awareness.*

Then pick people who have the talents, gifts, or skills you do not have. People who can fill in the gaps you do have. If you don't know yourself well, you will not pick the right people needed on your team. As a result, people will eventually be damaged or wounded from all the broken pointy pieces in your life. Treat the needs of others as sacred by knowing who you are — ASAP.

When dealing with yourself, commit to three things:

1. *get.*
2. *another.*
3. *pair of eyes.*

Often, we are our worst critics. We can benefit from another voice or two in our lives, to help see beyond our blind spots. Doctors do not diagnose themselves, attorneys do not represent themselves, and therapists do not counsel themselves. Generally, we are terrible at self-assessment. Reach out to a group of healthy friends, to help you see yourself better. People who know and care for you are your best safeguard between the two extremes of self-loathing and self-love.

We need all of you to be the best human beings possible.

Develop good HABITS.

Start today.

Start now.

 Begin to treat people the way you want to be treated. Showing care and compassion for others is one of the greatest things you can do on Earth. It's that simple.

STEP 6

SEEK COMMUNITY

Where do you seek community to find the best version of yourself?

"Life is not accumulation, it's about contribution."
-Stephen Covey

There is nothing so valuable, yet costs so little as a community. It is priceless and essentially free. Why don't more people take advantage of this remarkable face-to-face social phenomena? From politics and business, to churches and neighborhoods, almost every aspect of our lives is made up of some sort of community. There is a deliberately designed interconnectedness with others woven throughout our lives—and this interconnectedness helps us grow.

Anything that seeks to advance the progress of humanity happens in the context of community. Nothing of prolonged success or excellence is done in isolation. Medical breakthroughs, advancements in engineering or technology, space exploration, athletic achievements, innovations in business, education, and the arts—all of these require the combined efforts of a team. National movements such as Women's suffrage, the Green Initiative, Occupy Wall Street, Black Lives Matter, and the Civil Rights Movement have all etched a place in history, not because of a singular voice or visionary, but rather the collective passion and persistence of people who were part of a community.

Individuals are often celebrated as being the leaders of such movements, but those same leaders would not hesitate to tell the obvious: nothing happens in the context of "I," but everything great happens in the posture and power of "we."

Strength in Numbers

"If you have goals that can be achieved without the help of others, then you are dreaming too small."

Great leaders know the importance of community. They recognize that collaboration is the key to success. The saying, "It's lonely at the top," is misleading. Leaders who are at the top of their game are surrounded by talented groups of people strategizing and executing the vision. These leaders recognize that the greatest resource in their possession is not having exclusive knowledge, but being surrounded by committed human beings who will move the organization forward.

Community shatters the idea that a leader must have it all together and know what needs to be done at all times. Community commits to the process of leaders growing in deep and meaningful relationships with the people they lead. It is no longer vogue or cool to be perceived as the smartest person in the room, because the truth of the matter is: being the smartest is no longer good enough. An organization that seeks to advance a mission and goal bigger than itself will need creativity, passion, grit, determination, sacrifice, enthusiasm, clarity, wisdom, and resolve. It's difficult to find a person who has all of these characteristics individually, let alone all of them at once. But a community? A community will have all of these characteristics and more.

Community does not happen by chance or osmosis. It must be sought after, shaped, and formed. The final habit—Seek Community—is a clarion call, ringing from the depths of the human soul; a call to live the journey called life *with* others, and not alone. When leaders seek community, it is not a sign of weakness, but one of strength and wholeness. If you have goals that can be achieved without the help of others, you are dreaming too small. Any plan or idea with the capacity to advance the human spirit, to bridge divides between cultures, classes, and faiths — will require a collective effort.

The solution to such challenges will not come from the hands and hearts of one person. The challenges of our day demand leaders to work, seek common ground, and journey with others in order to pursue goals beyond the mundane. The dreams you have for your life, the life of your family, and the people entrusted to you all call for you to live in community rather than leading in a vacuum. There is too much at stake, and too little is gained by trying to lead and serve on your own.

Tuned Out

Earbuds are ubiquitous. People wear earbuds in all types of public spaces, including libraries, trains, coffee shops, buses, subways, gyms, and locker rooms. There was once a time when people wore earbuds in order to appreciate their music, but now it seems they are the must-have tools to keep people out. Out of our lives, our thoughts, conversations, hearts, and minds. Earbuds are a bit of a metaphor. We all have defenses we put up — earbuds, if you will — in order to stay detached and aloof from the hearts and hurts of people around us. Just as it is important to look up when someone is in your presence, it is imperative to take the earbuds out often. Too often, leaders attempt to lead from a place of detachment. But we were made to live in community, not in isolation. We must stop and realize that we need community not only to exist, but to excel beyond our wildest imaginings. And when you seek community, you don't look for ways to exclude others from your world; you embrace and make room for them.

The habit of seeking community is not a onetime exercise to avoid being alone. It is a commitment to align with others and to live life with them in a way that will not be task focused, but life giving. And yet, despite its benefits, many leaders remain aloof, distancing themselves from seeking and finding community. Maybe it is a matter of trust. With the competitive landscape today, the drive to be number one in your market can be stressful. However, the more closed off you become, the more quickly you set up your organization for failure.

"Set boundaries on your tendency to be a 'closed system,' and open yourself to outside inputs that bring you energy and guidance."
-Dr. Henry Cloud

In his book, *Boundaries for Leaders*, Dr. Cloud is a strong proponent of opening yourself up to receive input from others. Closed systems will die and closed people will become irrelevant. Being in receive mode allows leaders to continually grow. Getting to the top is only part of the picture; staying on top requires a strong commitment to community.

Powered On

"The average person will spend more than five years of their lives on social media."
Mediakix, 2017 Study

The advent of the internet and wireless technology has changed our daily lives in unimaginable ways. The mere thought of going through the day without our mobile phone, laptop, notebook, or e-Reader, is downright frightening. Whether we're on Facebook, Twitter, Instagram, or YouTube, it's hard to resist checking in several times a day to post our thoughts, and share information, photos, or videos. Instant access to real-time information and "going live" at the tap of a button—or even via voice activation— is exciting, addictive and time-consuming. According to a 2017 advertising study by Mediakix, time spent on daily social media use now surpasses time spent performing regular tasks such as eating, drinking, grooming, socializing and household chores. [22]

Social media advertising spending is in the billions of dollars, and those numbers will continue to rise. With our "must have" gadgets constantly gaining new and improved technological capabilities, and social media consumption increasing at warp speed, how do we find the time to step away and truly be part of community? It is a difficult balancing act. There are only so many hours in a day to get things done. It's easy to say that you will set boundaries and prioritize your use, but the addiction, the craving to be in the know and share information can be challenging, to say the least.

Of course, there are numerous advantages and disadvantages to social media use. For our purposes, the biggest disadvantage is that it takes away from community — that critical, healthy, one-on-one personal interaction with someone. Spending countless hours on social media is really a form of isolation. Even though you may be sharing public or private messages online, encouraging someone during a difficult time, a simple (actual, in-person) hug can do wonders to improve a person's emotional health. Community is important. It is a lifeline. Schedule time on your calendar to seek community in spite of your urge to post one more thing!

The Locals

The positive effects of being in a community environment can be seen neighborhood by neighborhood. Local community centers are the fabric of most municipalities. These centers offer everything from fitness programs and home improvement workshops to job training and parenting classes. People sign up by the hundreds to receive the benefits offered by their local community center. "Community" is the optimal word; it's where life happens. It's where people do life together, and discover life has so much more to offer when engaged on a journey alongside others.

Community centers aren't the only neighborhood program

where we see community being leveraged. In an attempt to better address relations between citizens and police during the late 1980s, law enforcement enacted community policing policies. In densely populated areas, officers no longer exclusively patrolled from their cars, instead they took to the streets to walk the beat in the neighborhoods. This led to police officers engaging in substantive conversations with residents and community leaders, from merchants to members of the clergy. Often, police officers held monthly forums at—guess where?—community centers, to hear from residents and work together to address neighborhood crime.

Early in the twentieth century, community colleges were established as a way to advance educational pursuits for people who were not necessarily prepared to leave home for the larger academic settings of universities and private colleges. A high school diploma wasn't necessarily enough to pursue career goals or meet the economic challenges of the day, and community colleges offered a way out for stay-at-home parents, minorities, and the skilled labor workforce. Diplomas from one- and two-year vocational programs, as well as pre-professional and technical fields were now within reach for residents in small towns and everywhere in between. Today, local counties, universities, municipalities, and faith institutions have all played a role in the development of community colleges.

More importantly, most churches today recognize how important it is for members of the congregation to gather outside of a Sunday morning service. Churches across the country and around the world offer groups where people meet in homes for Bible study and prayer, to share life experiences and break bread with one another on a regular basis. And what are these groups often called? Community groups.

Across many walks of life we see community being developed—communities formed around a common goal or interest, communities that seek to better themselves and others. To be clear, community is more than just having people around you in great numbers. Being part of a crowd is not the same as being part of and growing in community with others. Community goes beyond a mere gathering of people.

Authentic and vibrant community is not only a place that is devoid of judgement, but it's an environment that thrives on truth, openness, and honesty. Operating with a community mindset creates space for others to grow and reach their fullest redemptive potential. Community does not stunt growth and development, it encourages individuals to dig deeper to find fulfillment. When you're living in community your gifts and talents are celebrated.

A Time to Heal

As valuable as community is, the word itself has become overused. So let's think of it as a trusted circle of friends or advisers, or another pair of eyes. These types of groups can include someone who is wiser than you, like a mentor, or a parent, a group of friends and peers. Or better, someone who is unlike you in many ways, but is completely and absolutely in your corner.

Sarah was a young woman who had been abandoned by her father as a child. When she grew up, she embraced multiple lovers, multiple drugs, and multiple alcoholic blackouts. In one of those blackouts, she drove her car on the wrong side of a busy Los Angeles freeway, totaling her car and two other vehicles. Fortunately, no one was killed. She admitted that she once "booty-called" seven men at one time because she was lonely and bored. Most devastating was the fact that she stopped believing in love and settled for sex instead.

One afternoon, she ran into James, a family friend who'd known her as a child. They chatted briefly, and he invited her to church. A couple of months later, she showed up and sat in the back by herself, looking uncomfortable and alone; like a lost little girl. When people clapped or stood, she was motionless. James saw her across the room and came over to sit with her. Since she didn't stand, he didn't stand. Sarah didn't sing, so he didn't sing.

He just kept her company and said nothing. She sat through the entire service. Various people greeted her, and James introduced her as an "old friend." But later, Sarah slipped away without saying goodbye.

Later, James found out that Sarah had been walking home when one of the musicians from the church saw her. He and his family pulled over and offered her a ride home. She was quiet throughout the 20-minute ride, until they reached her home, when she politely thanked the driver and headed inside. James got the impression that she'd either disliked the whole experience, or just thought it was a waste of time. Fortunately, that wasn't the case.

Later, she told James that in that church, she felt so genuinely cared for, that it was overwhelming and almost uncomfortable. She wasn't used to that sort of treatment, and she didn't know how to respond. She sat there, motionless, in awe of a group of people who just cared for her with no hidden agenda. In the couple of years after that first encounter with a healthy community, Sarah got off drugs and alcohol. She got a steady job and kept it. She purchased a car and started dating a decent guy. That's the power of a community. It has the power to heal people.

There are millions of young people like Sarah who are waiting for you to invite them into your community. Like Sarah, Michael was a young man from a broken family. He was born to a teenage mother and a drug-addicted father with a long criminal record — a classic statistic with all the odds stacked against him. Today, Michael is a doctor, a respected professor and an executive in the law enforcement industry. How did this happen? He embraced community.

When Michael was younger he had significant mentors who invested in his life, drawing him into community projects where he lent a hand in helping others. As he matured, he took on the role of helping young people who came from similar circumstances to his own. He began working with churches and other community organizations, and for over 14 years, he was a part of projects to feed and clothe the homeless, provide shoes for needy kids, and to prevent sex trafficking. He often raised money for volunteer trips providing medical assistance and education in foreign countries. All of this happened in the context of a group with a common goal. A group of friends determined to make a difference. Friends and mentors sharing life, talking about what matters, sharing weaknesses in front of each other without judgment. Community.

Goodie:

There was a time in my life when I lived outside of community. It was a dark and lonely place. I made decisions and acted in ways that were inconsistent with God's best for my life. I was a shadow of what it meant to be a father, a husband, or a person who possessed the gift of leadership. I often felt like I was on the outside looking in—devoid of direction and purpose.

During that time, I was convinced that the pain in my isolation was a temporary feeling, and things would get better if I simply pushed through. Nothing could have been further from the truth. It never gets better when you are in isolation. It only gets darker as you become more isolated—for longer than is healthy for the human soul.

I remember there were days and weeks when I interacted with no one, had nowhere to be, and no one to care for, lead, or invest in. The phone did not ring, emails were few and far between, and there were no invitations to play pickup basketball or a round of golf. The silence in this season of isolation was deafening, and the inability to find my way forward left me void of passion, creativity, and to a degree, hope.

Some of the most difficult moments in my life have happened when I was serving, speaking, and leading hundreds and even thousands at one time. I failed to invest and put forth the effort to grow with others. When difficulties and challenges arose in my personal life and within the organizations I was a part of, I had nothing of substance to sustain the blows of challenge and frustration that occurred. In other instances, what I thought was community was simply a mirage at best—just make-believe.

I'm on the other side of that experience now, but the pain of isolation remains within. You can't spend time in the abyss of being alone and not have scars, emotionally or otherwise. My faith in God and the teachings modeled by the life of Jesus, as well as the love and care of my wife, children, and a handful of friends, brought me back in.

When I failed as a leader or did things out of character, I discovered that the relationships I'd formed were subject to me doing the right thing—and that's not community. You can determine the depth of your relationships not by how much people tell you they like you, but by how quickly they seek to move you towards healing, hope, and restoration. Community cannot be based on the words people say, but on the actions they take for your good.

One of the most unmistakable facets of community is that it has clear markings providing a way for you to return home. No matter how far away you've strayed from your true identity and purpose, you can always come home, like the prodigal son [23] or daughter. Mistakes that you made should not be regarded as periods at the end of your time in a community. Replace those periods with semi-colons which give you a chance to continue to write your story. In community, if you own up to your mistakes, seek to reconcile with God and others, you can start anew. When a relationship defines you not by your worst moments, but by your best—those relationships are worth keeping.

Melanie was in her late twenties. She was the most gifted, beautiful, yet broken person Tom had ever met. She had several scars on her body from self-injury. She had great parents, a loving sister and brother, and a close-knit extended family. She grew up in a good neighborhood and attended a top-notch school. Yet somewhere, for some reason, her life went off the rails.

The first time Tom met Melanie, she was in a psych facility under a 72-hour hold. What's a 72-hour hold? This meant that she self-injured, was given medical attention, and then *held* in a mental care facility for observation. Melanie's family had reached out to Tom and asked him to visit during those 72 hours. Sometimes he bought her a pack of cigarettes she wanted. Sometimes he just listened as she talked about her life. He offered a few words of encouragement and hope.

Once Melanie was released, Tom introduced her to his faith community and was intentional about introducing her to good people. She began to thrive. She proved to be hard-working, smart, and capable at whatever task she was given. Soon, she was hired to do various jobs for a local non-profit, which eventually turned into a full-time position. As her confidence grew, more of her talents, skills, and gifts came forward. In the sunlight of community, her previous moldy and unhealthy habits began to diminish and dry up.

Today Melanie is married to an extraordinary, loving man. She carries herself with a grace that belies the difficult years that she put herself (and all those who her loved her) through. How? Community had its way.

Let's not lose sight of the fact that community is not just for damaged or broken people. It's for high functioning and low functioning people—and everyone in between. A circle of friends or community is the most significant, helpful, healthy event that happens to us. It is a wonderful, unexpected gift. Therefore, it should be treasured and protected. Maintaining these types of deep friendships is hard work, but absolutely worth the investment.

The "D" Word

"It is time for parents to teach young people early on,
that in diversity there is beauty and there is strength."

-Dr. Maya Angelou

For several decades, the "D" word has been a subject of conversation and scrutiny in corporate America, politics, education, the arts, and sports. Diversity is rooted in civil rights legislation mandating that individuals from different cultures, genders, races, and religions are welcome in all societal arenas, and should be treated equally. The mere utterance of the word stirs up emotions and has varied meanings to those both directly and indirectly affected. Corporations have spent billions on diversity training. Has much changed in the workplace? In the arts? In education? You decide. Just read the headlines.

Today, it appears that we love the idea of *diversity*, but we lean towards *uniformity*. In thought. In dress. In beliefs. In demeanor. Take a look at your friends. Generally, you and your friends have similar political views, economic status, relational status. You probably live in similar neighborhoods, may even work in related industries. While we all long for our own uniqueness, and seek to live a non-cloned, non-standardized, original life, we still tend to find, befriend, and marry people like ourselves.

This is a primary reason to seek community. We all have blind spots—blind spots that are often reinforced by how we unknowingly gravitate towards people like us. But if you practice the habit of HABITS, diversity will organically follow. If you are a follower of the teachings of Christ and St.Paul, you know you are supposed to practice these HABITS. We, of all people, should naturally create diversity in relationships in our lives.

Now here's the tension of diversity in community: communities have mutual human interests. This is why some of the most interesting and healthy communities have common values, but diverse viewpoints. The people in these groups know each other, talk to each other, laugh with each other, care for each other, are *for* each other. They may not look alike, and they certainly don't see everything the same way. But they see *each other*.

It is in communities like this — of diverse viewpoints, backgrounds, and contexts — where we can find the most growth, if we acknowledge and embrace those differences for the new perspectives they bring to our own journeys. If you never wish to be challenged to live a courageous life, if you always wish to only be affirmed, if you do not want feedback or critique, then stay in your relational echo chamber. But if you want to grow, seek out a community you normally would not seek.

In her book *Salsa, Soul, and Spirit*, Juana Bordas speaks of the value of leadership emerging from three cultures: Native American, Hispanic, and African American. Borders asserts the core argument that leaders will need to be adaptable and flexible in a world that is constantly evolving with respect to diversity. Historic leadership modalities that derived from White or Anglo Saxon mindsets will not advance organizations or entities forward in a progressive society.

One of the many important insights Bordas raises deals with the power of community. She states that the Native American, Hispanic, and African American cultures model and value synergy, partnership, and the importance of journeying together on matters both significant and small. These insights are often overlooked when studying leadership. Yet so much can be learned if a correction is made in the academic and business communities who engage the study of leadership. Whether they are preparing a wedding feast, developing foreign policy, expanding profit share margins, or formulating a curriculum for a class — the leaders that will advance companies, families, churches, educational institutions, and businesses will be those operating from the understanding that more can be achieved in unity than in isolation.

We all stand on the shoulders of others. The idea that we can discover wisdom and insight on a solitary journey is a myth. We have our Greek philosopher friends to thank for that image, but it's a myth. All of us — regardless of our ethnic background, our socioeconomic status, or our education level — want someone to care about us. To know us. To see us. We are built for and function best in a community of friends.

Octavio:

My mother was raised in Durango, Mexico. She was the illegitimate child of a French diplomat and his 16 year-old housekeeper, my grandmother, *Ofelia*. My mother, *Maria Del Carmen Hernandez*, never received more than a 6th grade education. She and her half-siblings were poor. I mean poor. Dirt floors, communal well and outhouses. My mother had a flair for beauty — she was a looker, that Carmen — and she was driven.

Growing up in Mexico, she met a young, restless, reckless rake she would eventually marry: my father, *Octavio Gonzalez Martinez*. They came to America. Southern California specifically, Los Angeles exactly. My father, like many illegal immigrants, before him and many illegal immigrants, after him, entered the service industry to work as a dishwasher. He stayed in that restaurant industry while my mom stayed at home raising her three American-born kids.

My family lived in Huntington Park, a bedroom community of Los Angeles. When we moved into the the first and only home my parents ever bought, it was in an almost all-white community. But my parents had many friends, different types of friends: black, Mexican, Cuban, gay, white, straight, young and old. I can recall all of them at one point or the other visiting or eating at my home. But it was my mother's friend Mary Ellen — a black woman — and her husband, who prompted a lesson for me about people. My mother taught me there's more we have in common than not in common with people who are different from us.

Mary Ellen and my mother worked at the same place. She and her husband would come by the home at times to visit, as friends do. Once, when they did, some half wit driving past yelled, *"N- --lover!"* out their car window. Mary Ellen and her husband were mortified. My parents were angry. I do not recall what happened after that, or if they stayed, or how long they stayed.

What I do recall is what my mother told me afterwards: we're more alike than not alike.

Everyone.

All of us.

Ever since, I've noticed the common links which bind us all to each other. We are one species. Different cultures, different colors — but one species. Reality proved my mother was right again and again. The more people I got to know, the more I discovered again and again: we're *more alike* than *not alike*.

Remember: we're more alike than not alike.

If you want to succeed,

   If you wish to thrive,

      If you want to become a better human being,

        Seek community.

      And when you find one, stay in it.

      Even when it gets hard.

Community in Action

Kayla agreed to share her experience of community. This is her story in her own words: *"There is something about connecting with a genuine human being that is absolutely without a doubt the utmost important, transformative, healing thing for an individual who has experienced trauma or dysfunctional relationships at an early age.*

As a child of divorce and a home torn apart by a disconnect based on inability to fully understand and cope with the challenge of broken relationships, I left my home at 18 for a college across the country. I had no idea how to connect, relate, or feel safe or secure in any of my relationships. Was my family intentionally hurting me? No, but I had no one to exist with that truly knew how they felt about their relationship with self, others, and the world at large.

You did then and you do now.

You knew who you were down to the core of your being and you were confident enough in that relationship with yourself to know how to relate healthily with others and with the world. That is what I encountered here: a community of human beings that radically accepted their brokenness and worked daily to understand how that brokenness was meant to be transformative in their lives.

A community that loved themselves and loved others enough to say 'Hey, wherever you are in this walk called life, we are here to provide a safe and secure environment for you to figure it all out.' There was no judgment, no pressure, no rush. It was an open and honest energy that came from God. I had been jaded and turned off by so many Christians that I was skeptical and concerned as I sought out a church home.

I instantly felt my instinct stop me in my tracks here. I knew it was where I'd be given the opportunity to become more of who I was meant to be. It wasn't solely during my time in California that I learned this. It was in the years after, while I searched for a place that held that space for me again, that I realized what I had felt there.

Truly in my relationship with you and the rest of the congregation I felt the love of the in a Creator in a way I always searched for once I moved on. It was powerful! It was enough for me to feel the assurance that God lived, even in moments afterwards when I was in a very dark place."

God created us to be communal beings; interacting with each

other and doing things as a group. He first spoke of communion in Genesis 2:18 [24] when he said, "It is not good for the man to be alone. I will make a helper suitable for him..." God caused Adam to fall into a deep sleep and he took one of Adam's ribs and used it to create a woman, Eve. The joining of Adam and Eve expanded the roles of each as they embarked upon domestic and social life for the family unit as we know it. One thing is extremely clear, God said that being alone is not good. God is omniscient; he has full knowledge of everything. Take heed. You cannot reach your fullest potential without community.

Seek community. Don't settle for surface relationships. It's better to go deep with twelve people than muddle with a thousand in the shallows. Life presents enormous challenges and triumphs, and in either instance, we must surround ourselves with people who can thrive in whatever season comes.

Seek community.

BUILDING HABITS

A. Are you lonely?

B. Who knows you? Who would miss you?

C. Do you have a set of friends? Various levels of friendships? Friends who would sacrifice for you?

If you answered *Yes* to A, *No one* to B, or *No* to C, then consider trying these:

• Join a class to learn something new.

- Say yes to all social invitations.
- Invite someone out for coffee or dinner.
- Get involved with others who share your interests: political groups, places of worship, book clubs, or tours.

No matter what the circumstances, remember we are more alike than not alike. Seek community with others to bring out healthier personal and fulfilling relationships emotionally, physically and spiritually.

AFTERWORD

If you've read the entire book and made it this far, congratulations. Often, reading books like ours is one part helpful and two parts painful. Similar to receiving feedback from a close friend, we know it's good for us, but goodness it hurts a little too.

If you enjoyed this book, that may be because it confirmed for you what you intuitively knew. You did not have a name or title for your thoughts, and actions, but you had the *habit* of doing the right thing, in the right way, for the right reasons. Good for you my friend.

But let's say you are one of the ones who now sees why life has not been working for you in your personal and business relationships. The trajectory doesn't look good and instead of correcting course, you're doubling down with the same efforts which got you on this wrong path in the first place. Well, we still have good news: you *can* change course, you *can* become a different person, your past does not have to be your future because you get to write the last chapters. Remember, you never break a habit, you only change the habits you have. How long does it take to change or begin a new habit? About 21 days. So let's begin now.

Have Fun. Here's a good place to start. Who said work has to be miserable? What law requires us to not enjoy what we do? If you're not enjoying your job, your work, your career — your life — then change it. Start with you. No need to wait for external circumstances to change. Why? Because people are as happy as they choose to be.[25] And *you* are the one thing *you* have more control over than *anything* or *anyone* else. Have fun.

Assume the Best of Others. Most people start walking by placing their right foot out first. If you place your left foot out first, it feels odd. You're off balance. And, it'll take a few steps to correct, before you trip. People are like this. They start off by assuming the worst about someone and the relationship becomes awkward, off-balance, requiring more effort and time to correct, if they're able to do so at all. Practice the habit of Assuming the Best of Others and you'll find more pleasurable relationships.

Be Good Soil. Are you or do you know someone, who can quote all the right facts, know the right things and is talented, but cannot move forward in a positive manner? It seems they repeat the same mistakes over and over again? Sound familiar? If this is you, then change your soil. The problem isn't information. The problem is with our souls, minds, and emotions that prevents us from making healthy decisions. We don't need more information, we need to Be Good Soil.

Insist Upon Excellence. General Colin Powell is an amazing, gifted leader and public speaker. He is always enthralling, yet the most incredible aspect of his speeches is that he does not use notes. None. Yet he always hits on all eight cylinders. After multiple years of service and experience, he could "call it in" during his speeches and he'd still be better than most of us on our best days. Success is never given; it is earned. Do your best and bring your best everyday to each situation. Insist Upon Excellence.

Treat Others as Sacred. Of the many stories told of President Lincoln, the one where he always removed and tipped his hat when meeting children is the most charming. When asked why, he responded [paraphrased], "I know who the adults are, but I do not know who these children will become. I'm treating them accordingly." What if you created a culture in your personal and professional life of treating others as more important than yourself? What kind of organization would you have? Treat Others as Sacred.

Seek Community. This is an old proverb: *Without good direction, people lose their way; the more wise counsel you follow, the better your chances* (Proverbs 11.14). Still true. Help yourself and seek the company of a healthy community to speak into your life. All of us have blindspots and we need those extra eyes to tell us when we are violating our values, goals or moral codes. Who are your trusted friends, advisors and counselors? Seek Community.

ACKNOWLEDGMENTS

It is often said that the true measurement of one's wealth is not in the amount of money you have in the bank, the degrees you have mounted on a wall in your office, where you're from, or your last name. Instead, the true measurement of wealth is based upon the significant relationships you form. By all accounts then, I am one of the wealthiest human beings on planet earth.

Joshua C.H. Lewis Goodloe—you are my son, and I am well pleased with the young man you've become. Hannah Marie Goodloe—you are my daughter, and I am well pleased with the young woman you've become. I am so honored to be your dad! Ms. Lucy Goodloe—you are my wife and I am forever grateful that you said yes nearly twenty years ago, and that you continue to say yes, daily. Thank you for being my hero!

I would like to thank my mother, godmother, and grandmother: Mary Wagoner, Eugenia Franklin, and Leotha Coleman; my surrogate parents and mentors, Chester F. and Diana Stewart (thanks for embracing me as your son); as well as my mother-in-law, Mara Rosental; mentors Dr. J. Alfred Smith, Sr. and Lady Bernastine Smith Sr., Reggie and Dolores Lyles, Dr. Cheryl Elliott (mom, The Oracle), and friend Bobby Alexander (miss you Mr. A). Thank you to my esteemed colleagues and classmates at my beloved alma mater, Dallas Baptist University, in Dallas, Texas: President, Dr. Adam and Candice Wright; Chancellor, Dr. Gary and Sheila Cook; Provost Denny and Candice Dowd; Vice President for Financial Affairs, Matt and Karen Murrah; as well as Dr. James and Heather Byun, leaders and founders of Lifespring Church, Seoul, Korea, and Dr. Eric and Courtney Kuykendall (each of you are servant leaders personified). Thank you

Pastor Mike and Alice Goldsworthy and the entire community of Parkcrest Christian Church, Long Beach (I am grateful for your embrace of me and my family).

I am indebted to my professors and friends: Senator Fred Harris, Dr. F. Chris Garcia (The University of New Mexico), Dr. Mike Williams (Dallas Baptist University), Dr. Hak Joon Lee (Fuller Seminary, Pasadena, California), Ryan and Tawny Williams, Billy and Michelle Sanderson, John Martin Best, Reverend Elwood and Shirley McDowell; Soul Fruit: Toby Hill, Ty Covington, and Andres Adams; and solo artist, Vanessa Hill (cheering for you), Dr. Karen Eshoo; Angela R. Cannon; Kendall Hollinger, Michelle Carter; Coach Zac and Fawn Woodfin; Pastor Todd and Alice Salzwedel (First United Methodist Church, Odessa, Texas); Pastors Joshua and Noemi Chavez (7th Street Church, Long Beach, California; corazon y alma); Pastor J. Alfred Smith, Jr., and Allen Temple Baptist Church, of Oakland, California (#HindsFeet); Dr. Charles Becknell, Sr. of the Southern Christian Leadership Conference; Pastor Dave and Kara Bruskas (North Church, Albuquerque, New Mexico); Dana and Sam Ackland; Dr. Judy and Jeremy Yates; James and Francee Williams; David Smith; Pastor Mark Batterson; Carl and Lisa Winston Jr., Carl Winston III, & Carlissia Winston; Ken and Mary Watts; Ian, Kristen, and Luke Shelton; Pastor Stephen Brown and Dr. Nicole Brown; Dr. Tony Evans and Oak Cliff Bible Fellowship (Dallas, Texas); Keven "KC" and Zenobia Cook (heart and soul); Dr. Rodney Bennett, President of The University of Southern Mississippi, as well as the students, faculty, and staff of Presbyterian Christian School, Hattiesburg, Mississippi including Dr. Allen Smithers, Brian Smith, and Josh Dorman. A special thanks to the Leadership Lessons Series participants: Chief of Police for Long Beach, Robert Luna;Chris and Debbie Carlson; Cole Donahoo; Marcelo Voigt; Andrea Archambault; Shawn Martin; Roshan Maloney; and Ian Harris.

I want to acknowledge my former seminary president, the late Dr. Bill Crews (years ago he saw my God-given leadership gift); I am eternally grateful to my spiritual community: Steve and Sharon Kelly, Senior Pastors of Wave Church (spiritual and faith giants), and the entire pastoral and staff teams—I am honored to serve and help build the vision entrusted to you by The Transcendent (#WhatEverItTakes). A special thanks to my home church, Wave Los Angeles, and Pastors Israel and Rachel Campbell (#Onward). Finally, thanks to my team at Dream Life Loud, LLC: Kim Rouse (aka The Book Coach), Grace Mercer, Steven Albano, Karen A. Jones, Marcia Graham, and Jorgia Zvulon (#EditingSkills), and my co-author, Octavio Martinez—I hold you each in high regard.

Marcus Goodie Goodloe

****

There are many people who have contributed to, added to, spoken into my life. To the best of my ability, I've listed a few in alphabetical order: Michael Adnoff, Dr. Edward "Chip" Anderson, Jonathan Anderson, Eric Bryant Ph. D., Dr. David Ciocchi, Dr. Thomas M. Crisp, Alex Gilbert, Janine Goldsmith-Ripley, Dr. David Gonzalez, Dr. Marcus Goodloe, Joby Harris, John Huffman, Jean-Marie Jobs, Alex McManus, Erwin McManus, John Om, John Puls, Dr. Eddie Quan, Cory Shaw, Lisa Shaw, Dr. Gregg Ten Elshof, John Torres, Tom Taylor, and most of all... Rick Yamamoto.

Thanks to everyone who attended Sojourn and Mosaic Whittier; it was a wonderful journey, and lovely to experience; it was my privilege and pleasure to have been your pastor.

Anything beneficial in my life is the result of these men and women.

Mistakes were all mine.

Octavio Cesar Martinez

ACKNOWLEDGEMENTS

ENDNOTES

Step One: Have Fun

1. Cortisol is a steroid hormone that regulates the body's metabolism and immune system. Chronic stress can lead to high levels that have been linked to depression.

2. Apparently money can you buy happiness... at least up to $75,000.000 a year; after that money has little impact on happiness: Bonnie Kavoussi, "Money Improves Quality of Life, Up to a Certain Point," *Huffington Post*, April 18, 2012, https://www.huffingtonpost.com/2012/04/18/money-improves-quality-of-life_n_1434073.html.

3. Robert Barron, "Evangelizing Through Beauty," *Word on Fire*, 19 February 2013, www.wordonfire.org/resources/article/evangelizing-through-beauty/459/.

4. Sara Rimer, "The Biology of Emotion—and What it May Teach Us about Helping People to Live Longer," *Harvard Public Health*, Winter 2011, https://www.hsph.harvard.edu/news/magazine/happiness-stress-heart-disease/.

5. For more on the insights outlined here, see Melissa Etehad and Rob Nikolewski, "Millennials and Car Ownership? It's Complicated," *Los Angeles Times*, December 23, 2016, http://www.latimes.com/business/autos/la-fi-hy-millennials-cars-20161223-story.html.

Step Two: Assume the Best of Others

6. Alexandra Sifferlin, "Our Brains Immediately Judge People," *TIME*, August 6, 2014, http://time.com/3083667/brain-trustworthiness/.

7. See more of this story in the Gospel of John, Chapter 4.

8. 1 Peter 4:8

9. John Dear, *The Questions of Jesus: Challenging Ourselves to Discover Life's Great Answers* (New York: Doubleday, 2004), 45.

10. Ibid.

Step Three: Be Good Soil

11. Richard Feloni, "9 Timeless Lessons from the Great Roman Emperor Marcus Aurelius," *Business Insider*, February 9, 2016, http://www.businessinsider.com/lessons-from-marcus-aurelius-2016-2/#dont-spend-time-worrying-about-frivolous-people-who-have-no-positive-impact-on-others-1.

12. Paul Jun, "Seneca's Timeless Lessons on Friendship, Philosophy, and Self-Awareness," *Motivated Mastery*, July 23, 2013, http://motivatedmastery.com/seneca-life-lessons/.

13. Galatians 6:7

14. Marie Iannoti, "The Dirt on Soil," *The Spruce*, October 3, 2017, https://www.thespruce.com/the-dirt-on-soil-1403122.

15. Luke 8:4-10

Step Four: Insist Upon Excellence

16. Jenna Goudreau, "A Harvard Psychologist Says People Judge You Based on Two Criteria When They First Meet You," *Business Insider*, January 16, 2016, https://cdn.ampproject.org/c/s/amp.businessinsider.com/harvard-psychologist-amy-cuddy-how-people-judge-you-2016-1.

Step Five: Treat Others as Sacred

17. Tony Schwartz, "The Power of Community," *Business Insider*, September 5, 2014, http://www.businessinsider.com/the-power-of-community-2014-9/?r=AU&IR=T.

18. John 13:15

19. John 3:16

20. Philippians 2:3-5

21. John 20:24-29

Step Six: Seek Community

22. David Cohen, "How Much Time Will the Average Person Spend on Social Media During Their Life?" *Adweek*, March 22, 2017, http://www.adweek.com/digital/mediakix-time-spent-social-media-infographic/.

23. Luke 15:11-32

24. Genesis 2:18, 21-23

Afterword

25. "Folks Are Usually About as Happy as They Make Up Their Minds to Be," QuoteInvestigator.com, October 20, 2012, https://quoteinvestigator.com/2012/10/20/ happy-minds/.

Marcus Goodie Goodloe, Ph.D.

Goodie and his wife of twenty years, Lucy, live in the Los Angeles area and have two children, Hannah and Josh. Goodie serves as the Teaching Pastor at Parkcrest Church in Long Beach, California. In addition, he's actively involved with Wave Church in Los Angeles, California, where he leads the pastoral care ministry, and serves on the speaking team for the eight campuses of Wave Church, around the country.

A Compton, California native, Goodie travels the globe mentoring students and educators, business professionals, athletes and entertainers, and faith communities on issues including the dynamics of culture, human relationships, leadership, character development, and spiritual formation.

In 2011, he graduated from Dallas Baptist University with his Ph.D. in Leadership Studies. Goodie's dissertation was titled "Coalition of Conscience: An Assessment of Martin Luther King, Jr.'s Leadership with Athletes and Entertainers During the Civil Rights Movement, 1954-1968."

Following graduation, Goodie published his book, *Kingmaker: Applying Dr. Martin Luther King Jr.'s Leadership Lessons in Working with Athletes and Entertainers* in 2015. In 2016, Dallas Baptist University established the Marcus Goodie Goodloe Scholarship in his honor. He has served as a guest lecturer at several universities and seminaries. At present, he is an adjunct professor at Dallas Baptist University. He enjoys running, hitting a little white ball off a wooden tee, rooting for the Los Angeles Lakers, the Oakland Raiders (soon to be Las Vegas), and spending time exploring his options for good food.

Octavio Cesar Martinez

Octavio Cesar Martinez is an experienced sales manager, corporate relationship developer, and sales trainer, with more than 30 years of experience in the telecommunications industry. He has successfully designed and implemented sales and management training programs throughout Southern California.

Octavio shares his knowledge of leadership and personal development skills with people throughout the United States and around the world. He has addressed audiences and conducted seminars for businesses, colleges, churches and non-governmental organizations in Norway, Ecuador, India, Italy, Germany and Tajikistan.

Since his departure from full-time sales, Octavio has used his experience to conduct personal and corporate trainings in Scotland, Ireland, Italy, Germany, India, Tajikistan, Norway and across the United States. He has guest lectured at Fuller Seminary and BIOLA University; he has a degree in analytical philosophy with a minor in fine art and theology.

For three years, Octavio served as a Police Chaplain with two law enforcement agencies in Southern California. He was the founder of Mosaic Whittier, a spiritual community with a focus on personal development and the arts. Octavio is married with three adult children: David Octavio, Michael John and Christina Catherine; he currently lives in Southern California.

AVAILABLE NOW
PAPERBACK & E-BOOK

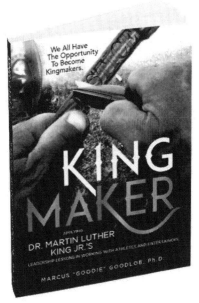

GET YOUR COPY TODAY!
AVAILABLE ONLINE
WHEREVER BOOKS ARE SOLD

OR ORDER DIRECTLY FROM
KINGMAKERMOVEMENT.COM

AVAILABLE NOW
PAPERBACK & E-BOOK

GET YOUR COPY TODAY!
AVAILABLE ONLINE
WHEREVER BOOKS ARE SOLD

Available at
amazon BARNES&NOBLE

OR ORDER DIRECTLY FROM
HABITSTHEBOOK.COM

AVAILABLE NOW

HABITS The Musical Journey.

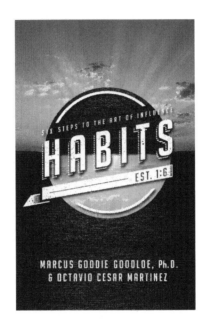

GET YOUR COPY TODAY!
AVAILABLE ONLINE
ON CD BABY.

NOTES

NOTES

Being confident of this,
that he who began a good work in you
will carry it on to completion until the day of
Christ Jesus.

Philippians 1:6 (NIV)

Made in the USA
Las Vegas, NV
17 October 2021